PROBLEM SOLVING TRAINING

for
Management and Supervisory Personnel

PROBLEM SOLVING TRAINING

Sessions Outlines
and
Reference Material

Training Within Industry Inc.
Cleveland, OH

Originally published as *Problem Solving Training: Sessions Outline and Reference Material*, released in 1944 by the War Manpower Commission of the Bureau of Training, Washington, District of Columbia.

Enna Products
1602 Carolina St.
Suite B3
Bellingham, WA 98229
Telephone: (360) 306-5369
Fax: (905) 481-0756
E-mail: info@enna.com

Cover Design/Illustrations by Khemanand Shiwram
Editor: Collin McLoughlin
Associate Editor: Shawna Gilleland

Library of Congress Control Number: 2009938939

Library of Congress Cataloging-in-Publication Data

United States. Bureau of Training. War Manpower Commission. 1944
     Problem Solving Training: Sessions Outline and Reference Material

     ISBN 978-1-926537-00-9
     1. Training Within Industry   2. Training of employees 3. Organizational change
4. Productivity–Increasing through training   I. Title

Dedicated to the men and women of The Greatest Generation.

CODE

CAPITALS . . . . Section Heads

Horizontal line across page . . . . Encloses section for timing

Plain type . . . . Trainer says in own words

★ Star in front of line . . . . Trainer says verbatim

Material between lines . . . . Board Work

Bracket . . . . Instruction to trainer

INTRODUCTION OF TRAINER

INTRODUCTION OF TRAINER

BY MANAGEMENT REPRESENTATIVE

The Directors of this Company want all of the Management personnel to be as well trained as possible in the duties and responsibilities of their work.

We realize that many day to day problems arise in your work that need wise and careful decisions before action can be taken.

This is one of your most important responsibilities.

The training program you are starting today will provide an opportunity to learn a simple and practical pattern to use in solving production problems.

The use of the skills learned in this program will be of the greatest value to you in developing a smooth running department.

We expect you to start using the skills learned here as soon as possible.

There will be eight, two-hour sessions and we expect you to attend every one and give your best attention and participation.

Let me present Mr. _____ who will conduct these sessions.

BEFORE THE SESSION STARTS

Give Management Representative a copy of "Introduction of Trainer" before the meeting.

Be in conference room 15 minutes before the session starts.

Be sure you have:

5 x 8 cards for names.

Hand out materials:

"Duties and Responsibilities of a Supervisor"

"An Outline for Solving Problems. Practice sheet #1"

"An Outline for Solving Problems. Practice sheet #2"

"Isolate the Problem. Practice sheet *3"

"Step 1"

Arrange chairs around table, or in U-shape if there is no table. Don't let members' first impression be that of a classroom.

Arrange to have facilities for hanging the charts.

Remember:

Have the right equipment, materials, and supplies.
Have the work place properly arranged.
Survey the blackboard.
Plan how you will space the board work.

MANAGEMENT INTRODUCTION

Follow outline.

OPENING THE SESSION

12 min

> Establish informal atmosphere and put the group at EASE.

GET ACQUAINTED

> Identify yourself. Explain your business and experience.
>
> Have each member tell the group something about his job, his company, and his responsibilities.
>
> To help members get started talking, ask such questions as:
>
> What are your responsibilities?
> How many people do you supervise?
> Are these people skilled or unskilled?
> Are they productive or non-productive workers?
>
> Use folded cards for displaying names and titles.

★ For the remainder of the program each member will
★ assume the position and responsibility of the title on
★ his name card.

THE SUPERVISOR, A MEMBER OF MANAGEMENT

★ In these meetings we will use the term "SUPERVISOR" a
★ great deal because our duties and responsibilities are
★ those of a Supervisor and we will be working with the
★ problems of a Supervisor.

★ Who are Supervisors?

★ For the purpose of our discussions when we refer to a
★ Supervisor, we mean anyone in charge of people, or who
★ directs the work of others.

(a) Includes: Foremen, Supervisors, Executives, Administrators.

(b) Includes: Group leaders.

(c) Includes: Some staff people, often referred to as functional Supervisors who have limited supervisory duties and responsibilities.

*12 min
to here*

DUTIES AND RESPONSIBILITIES

★ What are the Duties and Responsibilities of a Supervisor?

> Hand out "DUTIES AND RESPONSIBILITIES OF A SUPERVISOR".
>
> Discuss briefly.

★ What are some of the things that make your job unnecess-
★ arily difficult and keep you from getting out:

of good —	PRODUCTION
on —	QUALITY
at —	SCHEDULE
with —	LOWER COST
	SAFETY

> Develop answers from the group and place on the board.

Summarize:

★ Many Supervisors have never analyzed the causes of their
★ problems.

★ Some are uncertain what, if anything, can be done about
★ them.

★ Others feel strongly that someone else ought to solve them.

★ WHAT IS THIS ALL ABOUT?

★ I am not here to tell you how to run your business, but to
★ present a program which deals with the everyday product-
★ ion problems of a Supervisor, and a simple pattern to
★ follow for their solution.

★ Correct solving of production problems is one of the most
★ important duties and responsibilities of a Supervisor.

PROBLEMS

WHEN DOES A SUPERVISOR HAVE A PROBLEM?

A Supervisor has a problem when the work assigned fails to produce the expected results.

The elements of a job assignment:

Materials	Tools Equipment Machines	Standard operating procedures. Know-How	Performance

Materials	— Must be available.
Tools, etc.	— Must be proper and in place.
Standard Practice	— The best Know-How must be provided.
Performance	— Must be satisfactory and complete. It is not proper when something is "Out of Standard."

Standard. _____ Scrap

Tool Life.

WHEN PROBLEM SOLVING IS IMPORTANT

★ If the production problems are to be handled successfully,
★ the Supervisor must understand the fact that:

(a) Their problems are seriously interfering with their ability to get out production.

(b) Their problems have a direct effect upon Cost and Quality.

(c) Their problems are not necessarily inevitable.

(d) Their problems can be solved easily by following a definite pattern.

SUMMARY

Some production problems are small and fairly simple, and the Supervisor can solve them quickly by his experience and judgement.

Most production problems, however, are much more involved and important and cannot be solved quickly because the facts must be collected and analyzed before a decision can be reached.

PROBLEM SOLVING

★ In this program we learn by doing, therefore we will
★ practice on real production problems.

★ Let me tell you about a production problem that a certain
★ Supervisor had to solve.

> Pass out "Problem Practice Sheet #1" and explain its use here.

Tell the problem (Slowly and naturally).

"Smith, Supervisor of Department 'A', was walking through his department recently when he noticed three pans of angle plates on the floor in the main aisle. Smith called to a materials handler and reminded him that, "we must not leave material in the aisles, and besides Department 'B' was short of the plates."

Department 'B' Supervisor had reported not over an hour before that they would soon have to stop production if they didn't get the plates.

Smith asked his assistant why the plates were in Department 'A' and had not been moved out.

He replied that the Inspector said that some of them had over-size holes drilled in them.

Immediately Smith called the operator to his desk and reprimanded him for carelessness in his work. The operator complained that he had a sore finger, which he had cut on the pans while moving them.

> Members fill out the form. (Leader walks around group to give help where needed.)
>
> Sketch a similar form on the board.
>
> Develop the problem, using one of the member's sheets. Work with member individually.

4

If time permits repeat the practice with another member's sheet.

★ Summarize

Thank members for their participation.

This practice, though brief, seems to demonstrate that there is a need for further training in the techniques of production problem solving.

★ Now we will go one step further in our practice of solving
★ production problems.

Hand out 3 sheets of "Problem Practice Sheet #2" to each member.

Explain the sheet, its purpose and how to use it.

In using this form:

(a) Place an "X" in the small squares or circles to indicate the choice of your answer.
(b) Use simple short statements, not necessarily sentences, in filling in the large blocks.

Ask each member to think of a production problem and then to quickly fill in the form.

Have one member come to the head of the group with his problem sheet.

Have the member give his problem; Leader put same on board.

Ask, "Does the group have any questions about this problem?"

Leader to make brief comment on the problem and thank member.

Repeat same procedure with two other member's problems if time permits.

Summarize:

We are now aware of the fact that there is considerably more to solving production problems that was at first believed.

We seem to have difficulty in:

(a) Determining exactly what the problem is.

(b) Clearly giving proof of the problem.

(c) Stating the real cause, confusing it with evidence of the problem.

(d) Deciding what to do about it.

Thousands of Supervisors may, at this moment, be having difficulty in solving their production problems.

One is seldom born with this skill or technique but it can be easily acquired.

---

32 min **STEP 1—ISOLATE THE PROBLEM**

We will now take a look at a simple 4-step method which can be used by Supervisors to solve their problems at the Departmental level.

It is an easy, practical, and workable method.

> Develop titles of the 4 steps from the group and place on board.
>
> Present the 4 steps, titles only, on the board or by chart.

In this program we will take up each step separately, starting with Step 1, "ISOLATE THE PROBLEM."

> Hand out sheet on Step 1 and explain in detail.

1. State the Problem.

The problem is either MECHANICAL or PEOPLE or BOTH.
All problems involve people directly or indirectly.

PEOPLE who: Don't Know—Uninstructed or uninformed.
Can't Do—Unable physically or mentally.
Don't Care—Lacking in interest or initiative.
Won't Do—Insubordination. "Problem worker."

2. Give Proof or Evidence of the Problem.

Statistical data to prove there is a problem, about the:

MECHANICAL part of the job: Quality, Equipment, Tools, Safety, etc.

6

PEOPLE involved in the job: Their habits, skills, attitudes, productivity, etc.

3. Explore the Cause.

When the cause is determined it is easier to make corrections.

The cause may be:

MECHANICAL: Methods, Layout, Machines, Tools, etc.

PEOPLE with: Wrong assignment, Faulty instruction, Personal problem or human relations, Insufficient skill or experience.

> To show relationship between #2 and #3, above it is helpful to ask such questions as: Why did this happen? Where? When? Who is responsible?

4. Draw conclusions.

From the above facts we now know exactly what the problem is, and its cause or causes. We are now ready to prepare for its solution. Before presenting the details on how to prepare for a solution we will now take necessary time to gain skill in the use of Step 1 "Isolate the Problem" through actual practice.

1 hr
40 min
to here

---

25 min **STEP 1—PRACTICE**

> Hand out "Problem Practice Sheet #3" (3 or 4 to each member).
>
> Explain the sheet in detail.
>
>   Take each step and item separately.
>
>   Use examples for fuller explanation. Use board for emphasis.
>
>   Show relationship between "Proof or Evidence" and "Cause."

1 hr
55 min
to here

---

5 min **ASSIGNMENTS FOR THE NEXT SESSION**

> Each member to bring in a production problem with Step 1.
>
> Have "Isolate the Problem" analyzed completely on Problem Practice Sheet #3, and be ready to explain the details of it to the group.

In order to assure variety in problems and to have practice in problems of different types, divide the group so as to cover the following types of production problems:

Quality problems   — Scrap, rework, tool breakage, etc.

Quantity problems — Schedule-trouble, "bottlenecks."

Safety problems   — Increase of accidents.

Cost problems   — Labor or material cost up.

People problems   — Productivity low, work habits bad.

★ Does everybody understand their assignments?

Briefly review what has been covered in this session.

Duties and responsibilities of a Supervisor.

Problems of a Supervisor.

Problem solving of production problems.

4-step method.

Step 1 "Isolate the Problem."

Assignments.

Thank members for their cooperation and interest.

BEFORE THE SESSION STARTS

Be in the conference room 15 minutes before the session starts.

Have everything ready. This Includes:

> Tables and chairs properly arranged.
> Blackboard clean and ready for use with chalk and
>   eraser.
> Supply of "Problem Practice Sheet #3" on hand.
> Chart: Step 1 and Step 2.

OPENING SESSION II

Make appropriate remarks. Welcome the group.

Review the first session briefly.

"Problem Solving," an important responsibility of Supervisors.

Discuss some common production problems.

List the 4 steps (Titles only) on board or by heart.

Review Step 1—"Isolate the Problem"

10 min
to here   Select three problems from group to use in this session.

---

30 min **DEMONSTRATION OF STEP 1**

★ For the next hour and a half we will get practice in the
★ use of Step 1, "Isolate the Problem." There will be three
★ demonstrations.

★ We will now start with the first demonstration.

Pass out "Problem Practice Sheet #3" to members (3 or 4
each).

Ask member with 1st problem to come to the head of the table,
bringing his problem sheet with him.

★ Please tell your problem to the group.

After he has finished, ask the group:

★ Is this a production problem? (Get agreement)

★ Is this a "Mechanical" problem? (Get agreement)

Place an outline on the board similar to that of the "Problem
Practice Sheet #3."

Fill in form on board exactly as the "Supervisor" gives it.

★ Please fill in your form as it is on the board.

Ask the "'Supervisor":

★ What does this problem concern?

★ Exactly what is your problem?

11

★ What proof or evidence do you have of this problem?

★ What have you checked under, "Explore the Cause"?

★ Which circle did you check under, "Conclusion"?

★ Is this form on the board filled in the same as your sheet?

> Review the problem briefly.

★ Let's now give the members a chance to ask questions.

> Refer to the "Supervisor" for all answers, he is the expert.

★ If this were your problem how would you have filled in
★ the spaces?

★ Do you think this form is filled in completely?

★ Do you think that the problem, as stated, is really correct?

Conclude:

★ Before we can proceed to solve this or any production
★ problem we must be sure that we know exactly what
★ the problem is.

★ "Isolating the Problem" as done in this demonstration was
★ better than is found in most industries today.

★ It did however bring out the important point that the time
★ and study necessary to "Isolate the Problem" must be done
★ before proceeding to the solution of the problem.

★ Are there any questions?

> Thank the member and have him return to his seat.

---

30 min SECOND DEMONSTRATION OF STEP 1

★ We will now have the second practice demonstration of
★ Step 1.

> Have member come to the head of the table with his problem
> sheet.

Please tell your problem to the group.

Draw form on the board similar to that of "Problem Practice Sheet #3."

Fill in the form as follows, exactly as the "Supervisor" gives it.

Do not check the top circles now.

In the proper space fill in "Exactly what the problem is."

In the proper space fill in "Proof or Evidence of the problem."

Instruct group members to fill in their sheets as follows (allow 3 min.).

Check the proper circle at the top.

Check the squares under "Explore the Cause."

Have the "Supervisor" continue as follows: (Check same on board)

Tell which circle he checked at the top.

Tell what squares he checked under "Explore the Cause."

Tell what circle he checked under "Conclusion."

Let's again give the members a chance for questions and comment.

Ask the following types of questions: (refer answers to "Supervisor")

What type of problem was this?

Did you have your sheet marked differently? What differences?

Do you believe that we have the problem completely isolated?

Conclude:

Again we can see how necessary it is to determine exactly what the problem is. Without this we should not proceed.

Thank the "Supervisor" and have him return to his seat.

THIRD DEMONSTRATION OF STEP 1

We will now have the third practice demonstration of Step 1.

> Have a member come to the head of the table with his problem sheet.
>
> Draw form on the board similar to that of "Problem Practice Sheet #3."

Please tell your problem to the group.

> After he has finished, fill in the following exactly as he has it:
>
> "Proof or Evidence of the Problem" (Only this space at this time).

Please fill in your form for this problem as you think it should be (Allow 5 minutes).

Check circles at top of the form.

Check squares under "'Explore the Cause."

Write in your own words, "Exactly what the problem is" in proper space.

> Compare answers of the members of the group. Check these with the "Supervisor"; he is the "expert." Ask members the following questions:

What circle did you check at the top of the sheet?
Why?

What squares did you check under "Explore the Cause"?
Why?

What did you have in the space, "Exactly what is the Problem"?
Why do you believe this is correct?

Did we have any other answers in this space? Why?

> Again turn to the "Supervisor" for his answers from his sheet.

Please tell what you have in the vacant spaces as I write them on the board.

Thank the member and have him return to his seat.

Conclude:

We can see how difficult it is to be certain of the problem.

We often think we know when we really don't.

We may know the circumstances so well that we don't plan on any exact method of solving it.

1 hr
40 min
to here

Experience shows that more time and consideration should be given to the details before considering how to prepare for the solution.

---

10 min **DEVELOP STEP 2 HEADING**

★ We now have had practice on the skill of "Isolating the
★ Problem" and are ready to go on to Step 2.

Place Step 1, "Isolate the Problem" on the board.

★ How many remember the title of Step 2? (Develop from group)

Place Step 2, "Prepare for Solution" on the board under Step 1.

★ This step is now divided into two general types of
★ problems.

★ What do you think they are? (Place answers on board)

1 hr
50 min
to here

Place the exact heading on the board, or use chart.

---

10 min **ASSIGNMENTS FOR SESSION III**

★ So that we may learn by doing, we now will make two
★ assignments for Session III.

Assign to two members:

★ Bring in problems of a "MECHANICAL" nature. The
★ problems dealing with Methods, Layout, Equipment,
★ Tools, Materials, or Machines.

15

⌐ Explain exactly what is wanted: ⌐

   Step 1 filled in completely.
                                    ⌐

★ Be prepared to go further into details carrying the problem
★ into the production line itself. Make it a real production
★ problem.

⌐ Review what we have done in the sessions to date. ⌐

★ We are now ready to learn how to prepare for the solution
★ of production problems. The details will be brought out in
★ the next session.

BEFORE THE SESSION STARTS

Be in the conference room 15 minutes before the session starts.

See that chairs and tables are properly arranged.

Have everything ready.

Have the following "hand-out" material ready in sufficient quantity so that each member may have the following amount:

Step 2 Complete Outline	1 per member
Step 2 Mechanical Problem Solving Outline	1 per member
Flow Chart sample	1 per member
Flow Chart blanks	5 per member
Flow Diagram sample	1 per member
Flow Diagram blanks	5 per member
Methods Breakdown sheet sample	1 per member
Methods Breakdown sheet blanks	5 per member
Definition of Symbols	1 per member
"Parachute"	1 per member
The three parts of a Job	1 per member

Following charts (if to be used):

Step 2
Make a Flow Chart
Symbols
Question the Job as a Whole
The Flow Diagram
Make a Methods Breakdown
All Jobs are Divided into Three Parts
Types of questions

OPENING OF SESSION III

Greet members cordially.

Make appropriate remarks.

Review Session II. Display Session II chart.

Discuss the Problem Practice Sheet #3 briefly.

Importance of isolating the problem before continuing.

Check on assignments; select problems to be used in this session.

5 min
to here

---

8 min ## STEP 2—PREPARE FOR SOLUTION

★ We are now ready to learn how to "Prepare for Solution"
★ of production problems.

★ For the ease of understanding and handling, we divide
★ all production problems into two general types:

MECHANICAL: such as those involving...

Methods

Layout

Tools

Equipment

Materials

Machines

PEOPLE: who...

Don't Know

Can't Do

Don't Care

Won't Do

Hand out "Step 2, Prepare for Solution."

Display chart of same. Explain headings.

★ The remainder of this session will be devoted to detailed
★ study of those problems that commonly can be called
★ "MECHANICAL." The other parts of this Step will be
★ presented later in Session III.

Conclude:

We know that all production problems involve PEOPLE either directly or indirectly, however in our everyday production work we seem to have many problems that are apparently "MECHANICAL" in nature such as:

Quality	—	Scrap, Rework, Spoilage, etc.
Quantity	—	Schedule, Bottlenecks, etc.
Safety	—	Unsafe conditions and situations, etc.
Cost	—	These all increase cost.

OUTLINE: SOLVING MECHANICAL PROBLEMS

★ We now present an outline of the solving of MECHANICAL
★ problems.

> Hand out "Mechanical Problem Solving Outline" sheets.
>
> Display chart of same and explain the points listed below:

★ When the problem is MECHANICAL.

involving …	
METHODS	ANALYZE THE OVERALL JOB OR SITUATION
	Make a Flow Chart.
	List routing or travel of a part, material or paper.
LAYOUT	Show relationship to prior and subsequent operations or situations.
	Question the job or situation as a whole.
	Make a Flow Diagram.
TOOLS	Show layout and locations of work stations, equipment, aisles, etc.
	Study for better production efficiency and for possible causes of problems.
MACHINES	ANALYZE SPECIFIC JOB OR SITUATION
	Make a breakdown of the method of doing the job or of the situation.
	List all details including:
EQUIPMENT	Materials handling
	Machine work
	Hand work
	Question all details to help locate problem sources.
MATERIALS	Use: WHY, WHAT, WHERE, WHEN, WHO, HOW.

*20 min
to here*

MAKE A FLOW CHART

★ Experience shows that a Flow Chart can be used advanta-
★ geously when studying a situation where a change is
★ contemplated, or a problem exists.

★ It shows the routing of the subject and its relationship to
★ prior and subsequent operations, inspections, handlings,
★ delays, and storages.

★ The subject may be a part, assembly, material, paperform,
★ etc., but usually it is a part, as most problems occur to
★ mechanical things.

★ One of the important sections of a Flow Chart is the "Sym-
★ bols" section. They are used to graphically show what is
★ happening to the subject.

★ Extra emphasis is obtained by drawing a connecting line
★ from symbol to symbol thus highlighting costly items like
★ handlings, delays, storages, etc. Colored lines or symbols
★ can be used for further emphasis if wanted. Definitions of
★ the meaning of symbols used is found on the next page.

Here is a quick, easy way to make a Flow Chart:

1. Fill in headings.
2. Fill in "Subject charted".
3. List what happens to the subject charted.
4. Give "Oper. No." where it applies.
5. List "Dept." in which it occurs.
6. "Distance" in feet for transportations.
7. "Time" for all delays.
8. Apply symbols and connect dots.

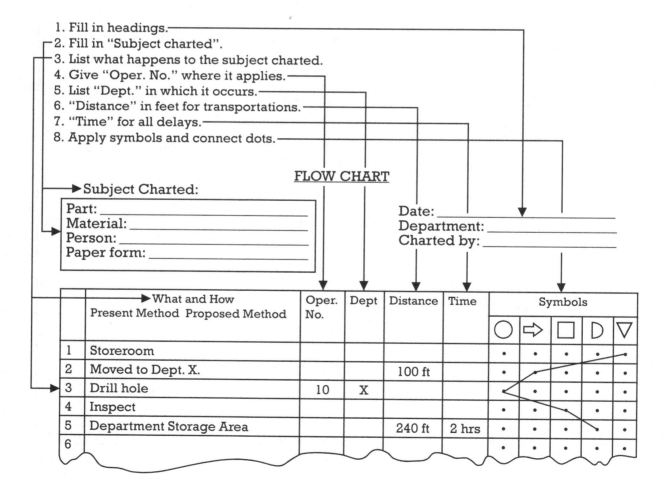

FLOW CHART

Subject Charted:

Part: _____
Material: _____
Person: _____
Paper form: _____

Date: _____
Department: _____
Charted by: _____

	What and How Present Method Proposed Method	Oper. No.	Dept	Distance	Time	Symbols ○	⇨	□	D	▽
1	Storeroom					•	•	•	•	•
2	Moved to Dept. X.			100 ft		•	•	•	•	•
3	Drill hole	10	X			•	•	•	•	•
4	Inspect					•	•	•	•	•
5	Department Storage Area			240 ft	2 hrs	•	•	•	•	•
6						•	•	•	•	•

STANDARD DEFINITIONS OF SYMBOLS

Hand out "Definitions of Symbols" and explain (Use chart).

<u>Classification</u>	<u>Symbol and Definition</u>

Operation

An operation occurs when:
(a) An object is intentionally changed in any of its physical or chemical characteristics.
(b) It is assembled or dissembled from another object.
(c) It is arranged or prepared for another operation, transportation, inspection, or storage.

An operation also occurs when:
(a) Information is given or received.
(b) Planning or calculating takes place.

Transportation

A transportation occurs when an object is moved from one place to another, except when such movements are a part of the operation or are caused by the operator at a work station during an operation or an inspection.

Inspection

An inspection occurs when an object is examined for identification or is verified for quality or quantity in any of its characteristics.

Delay

A delay occurs to an object when conditions, except those which intentionally change the physical or chemical characteristics of the object, do not permit or require immediate performance of the next planned action.

Storage

A storage occurs when an object is kept and protected against unauthorized removal.

Combined Activity

Operation-Inspection   Storage-Inspection

When it is desired to show activities performed either concurrently or by the same operator at the same work station, the symbols for these activities are combined.

QUESTION THE JOB AS A WHOLE

★ We question the job or situation as a whole from the Flow
★ Chart, which is usually the starting point in the process of
★ making any improvement or when solving production
★ problems. It will highlight such costly and troublesome
★ items as Transportation, Inspections, Delays, Materials
★ Handling, Safety Hazards, etc.

★ Let's consider the prerequisites for proper questioning.

★ 1. Have an open mind.

The mind is like a parachute; it functions only when open.

Cultivating an open mind is difficult, but it is absolutely necessary if you expect to find openings for improvements and for solving production problems.

★ 2. Develop and maintain a questioning attitude.

Your success in preparing for the solution of production problems depends on the ability to develop a questioning attitude.

Question everything. Never accept any job as being perfect.

The answers you get will give the information you need. The more thorough the questioning, the better the facts.

Beware of mental road blocks.

The greatest obstacle to probing for causes of problems is not created by technical difficulties, but rather it is set up by the mental attitudes of people who feel that they already are using the least troublesome methods.

It has often been said that tradition destroys progress. Just because a job is done in a certain way is no proof it is the best way.

Just because a job is done at all is no proof that it is necessary.

The fact that the method of doing the job has been in effect for years is no proof that it is the best way.

★ The best results are obtained by asking:

WHY is it necessary? WHAT is its purpose? Can it be eliminated? Can it be Combined in whole or in part with another operation? Can it be Rearranged in routing or sequence? This would save: Handlings, Back-tracking, and Delays and also improve working conditions.

★ If this questioning process reveals the answer to the
★ problem then record it on:

Flow Chart for the corrected or proposed method.

---

10 min **THE FLOW DIAGRAM**

★ We will now discuss the Flow Diagram and its use in
★ solving production problems.

★ The Flow Diagram is a simple graphic picture of an area,
★ on which is shown the movement of an item.

Actually follow the item or subject, keeping to area involved.

Detail or indicate every: Operation, Transportation,
Inspection, Delay, or Storage.

Flow Diagrams are helpful in visualizing the situation when
studying and planning for efficient manufacturing and in solving production problems.

Here is an example of a simple Flow Diagram.

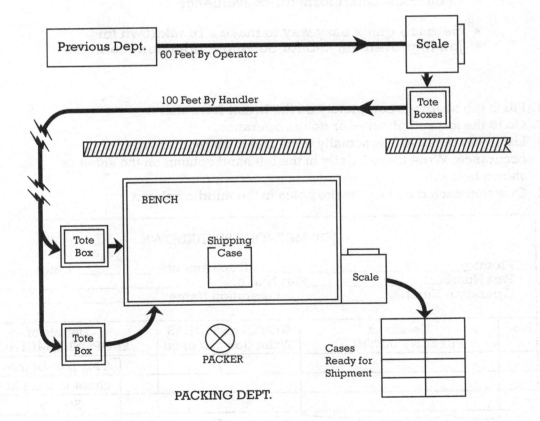

Pass out sample Flow Diagram and explain.

25

BREAKDOWN THE SPECIFIC JOB

★ Refer to "Outline for Solving Mechanical Problems" (Chart).

★ We have analyzed the overall job or situation in search of
★ the answer to our production problems.

★ In this analysis we may have found the answer, but more
★ often we learn that it is a "Specific Job or Situation" in
★ which the trouble is located.

★ We will now practice analyzing the specific job or situation.
★ This is done by:

   1. Breaking down the job
   2. Questioning every detail

BREAKDOWN THE JOB

★ Breaking down the job into steps or details gives us facts.

★ The breakdown sheet is a complete and accurate record of
★ the operation or job. This should be made on the job as it
★ is actually done *Just as you See it*, not as you remember it.

★ We often place this breakdown form on the opposite side
★ of the Flow Chart form for convenience.

★ Here is a quick easy way to make a breakdown for
★ Job Improvement and for Solving Production Problems.

1. Fill in the headings completely on the breakdown sheet.
2. Go to the job and observe or do the operation.
3. List every detail as it is actually done and in its regular order of
   occurance. Write these briefly in the left hand column on the sheet as
   shown below.
4. Question each detail and make notes in the middle column.

JOB METHODS BREAKDOWN

From: _____ Department: _____ Date:_____
Part Number: _____ Part Name: _____
Operation Number: _____ Operation Name: _____

No.	Details of PRESENT METHOD	NOTES and IDEAS Write down at once	Details of PROPOSED METHOD	
			This part of the	
			sheet is used in	
			Step 3.	

THREE PARTS OF A JOB

★ From our analysis we believe the trouble or problem lies
★ in a specific job or location.

★ To locate or discover it we must use the questioning
★ process.

★ Experience shows that the source of many production
★ problems lies in the handling or movement of parts of
★ materials.

★ Movement of material without definite work accomplish-
★ ment is either:

(Chart)   MAKE READY
                                           PUT AWAY
                                           WASTE

MAKE READY This is the time and effort spent in getting things ready, such as: Materials, Tools, Equipment, and Gauges. Also the placing of the material or part in the nearby work area, from trucks, pans, racks, etc.	
	**DO** This is the work that actually accomplishes the desired main objective and does add to the value of it. e.g. Drill a hole, Plane a board, etc.
PUT AWAY This includes all details necessary to complete the job after the "DO" operation. It includes setting the part aside and/or placing on trucks, in pans, on racks, on conveyors, etc.	

★ The greatest opportunity for improvement, or the disc-
★ overy of the source of a problem is in "MAKE READY"
★ and "PUT AWAY."

★ They add to the time and cost but not to the value of the
★ end product. Less than 50% of the total time is usually
★ consumed by the "DO" part of the Job.

---

10 min ## QUESTION EVERY DETAIL

The "DO" details are questioned first because if they are unnecessary, or if the answer to the problem is here, then there is
no need to question the rest of the operation. Otherwise continue the questioning in the regular manner.

The "MAKE READY" and "PUT AWAY" details afford the greatest opportunity for improvements and discovery of problem
causes.

<u>Types of questions to be asked:</u>   (Chart)

<u>WHY IS IT NECESSARY?</u>
We ask this question of each detail to distinguish necessary details from those that are unnecessary, doubtful, or
troublesome.

This is the most important question and the hardest to get answered.

<u>WHAT IS ITS PURPOSE?</u>
This is the check question to WHY is it necessary. We
want to learn if the detail has a useful purpose or adds to
quality. If it does not, we will reconsider its necessity.

If the detail is found to be necessary, then continue with other
question, as follows:

<u>WHERE SHOULD IT BE DONE?</u>
Where is the best place or location to do the detail?
Why is it done there? Where else could it be done?
Could it be combined with another detail?
Could this be the location of the problem?

<u>WHEN SHOULD IT BE DONE?</u>
We ask this question to find the best time to do each detail. What details must it follow, and what detail must it
precede? Why is it done at this time? Are the details in
proper sequence? Can it be done simultaneously with
another? Could the timing be the cause of the problem?

<u>WHO IS BEST QUALIFIED TO DO IT?</u>
We ask this question to learn who is best qualified from
the standpoint of skill, experience or physical strength.
Is the source of the problem here?

<u>HOW IS THE BEST WAY TO DO IT?</u>
We ask this question only after asking WHERE?, WHEN?,
and WHO? Can it be done easier and safer? Can the layout of the work-station be improved? Are proper tools

and equipment used? Can this be the source of the problem?

List your IDEAS and THOUGHTS arising from these questions, on the breakdown sheet in the column marked "NOTES and IDEAS." It is from these that the new method or correction is developed.

PRACTICE DEMONSTRATION

★ We have presented the outline for solving MECHANICAL
★ Problems.

★ What is necessary to do this?

> Place quickly on board—have brief comment.

> Make a Flow Chart of Overall Job
> Make a Flow Diagram of area if needed
> Make a Job Breakdown of Specific Job
> Question details to find facts upon which
> we can make corrections

★ These are the facts with which you can proceed to make
★ the correction. This will be presented in SESSION V.

> Draw a sample blank Flow Chart on the board.

★ Now let's do a practice problem.

> Pass out blank Flow Charts to group.

★ Please copy on your form what I put on the board.

★ I will now tell the problem (same one used in SESSION I)

★ I have the problem worked out on the Step 1 form.

★ It shows the problem to be MECHANICAL.

> Fill in the Flow Chart form on the board from the sample Flow Chart.
> Review briefly—Ask if there are any questions.

★ What do we do next?

Question the overall Job.
Ask members for types of questions.
List or note their answers.
Brief comment.

Conclude:

★ We have done the first thing but we do not seem to have
★ found the specific facts upon which we can make a correc-
★ tion of the problem.
★ We do have a step here which should be analyzed further.

★ Which one is it? (Brief discussion)

★ Do you think we should make a Flow Diagram in this case?
★ Why? (Brief discussion)

★ What should we do next in gathering facts so we can make
★ a correction?

Draw out from group—Brief discussion.
Answer—Breakdown Specific Job.

★ Let's make a Job Breakdown of the specific job.

Pass out blank breakdown sheets.

★ Copy on these sheets as I place the breakdown on board.

Draw a Job Methods Breakdown Sheet form on board.

Copy the breakdown from the sample sheet of the job.

★ Which is the "DO" detail? (brief discussion)

★ Which are the "GET READY" details? (brief discussion)

★ Which are the "PUT AWAY" details? (brief discussion)

★ Which detail do we question first? (Answer—a "DO" detail)

Have a member question—(coach him)
Ask for group comment.

★ Do we find facts here that can be used in making the
★ correction?

★ What details do we question next? (Answer is "GET
★ READY")

> Have a member question these details—(coach him)
> Ask for group comment.

★ Do we find facts here that can be used in making the
★ correction?

> Discuss "Bring out Facts." List on board.

★ What details do we question next? (answer is "PUT
★ AWAY")

> Have a member question these details—(coach him)
> Ask for group comment.

★ Do we find facts here that can be used in making the
★ correction?

> Bring out the fact that the drill was dull and it was running at
> too high a speed.

Conclude:

This brief problem points out the general use of this easy, simple procedure to help prepare for the solving of MECHANICAL problems.

5 min **MAKE ASSIGNMENTS**

> Make Assignments.

★ We have covered the MECHANICAL problem solving part
★ of Step 2 but you may remember that the problem may not
★ always be Mechanical.

★ What other types of problems may there be?

> Refer to Chart—Discuss briefly.

★ We will present this angle in the next session.

★ We will need some problem to practice upon.

★ Who will bring in a problem where the trouble is due to
★ Faulty Instruction? Bring in this problem with Step 1 form
★ filled in.

★ Who will bring in a problem where the trouble is due to a
★ Personal situation or Human Relation situation?
★ Bring in Step 1 form filled in.

Thank group for interest and participation.

BEFORE THE SESSION STARTS

Be at meeting room 15 minutes before Session starts.

Have everything ready:

Chairs and tables properly arranged
Blackboard ready —
Hand-outs ready —

Sample Job Instruction Sheets	1 per member
Blank Job Instruction Sheets	2 per member
Sample Relations Problem	1 per member

Chart — Step 1
Chart — Step 2
Chart — Get Ready to Instruct
Charts — Job Instruction Sheet Presentation
Charts — Time table Presentation
Charts — Job Relations Presentation

OPENING OF SESSION IV AND REVIEW

Greet members.

Review: Step 1—Use chart—brief discussion
            Step 2—Use chart—brief discussion

MECHANICAL PROBLEMS

(a) Overall Job
        Flow Chart
        Flow Diagram
        Question Overall Job

(b) Specific Job
        Break Job down into details
        3 parts of a Job
        Question the details

Now we will take up the "PEOPLE PROBLEM" part of this step.

Remember, not all problems are MECHANICAL in nature. Most of them are PEOPLE problems.

    due to: ===============

            Faulty Instruction
            Wrong Assignment
            Personality Situation

                    ===============

Or, in other words—People who:

                ===============

            Don't Know
            Can't Do
            Don't Care
            Won't Do

                ===============

PROBLEMS DUE TO FAULTY INSTRUCTION

★ First we will devote our time to "PEOPLE PROBLEMS" due
★ to "Faulty Instruction."

★ What is "Faulty Instruction"? | Place answers on board. |

> Insufficient Instruction
> Incorrect Instruction
> Inefficient Instruction
> No Instruction

★ What can be the cause of "Faulty Instruction"?

> Little or no preparation of:
>
> Work Place
> Instructor
> Learner

★ To prepare for the solution of production problems
★ resulting from Faulty Instruction we must:

> GET READY TO INSTRUCT

| Present "Get Ready to Instruct." |
| Use board or chart—Discuss briefly. |

Get Ready to Instruct

(1) Prepare the Workplace
   Have everything ready
   Have the workplace properly arranged

(2) Prepare yourself
   Make a Job Instruction Analysis
   List Important Steps
   List Key Points
   Plan the Instruction
   Make a Time Table
   Who will do What, When, How soon?

(3) Prepare the Learner
   Put him at ease
   Find out what he knows about the job
   Interest him in learning the job
   Position him correctly for instruction

We will now take up each part separately

(1) <u>Prepare the Workplace</u>

(a) Have everything ready —

MATERIALS	EQUIPMENT
TOOLS	SUPPLIES

Ask questions—get brief discussion.

★ What should be ready in your department?

★ What problems might arise if everything is not ready?

★ Who is responsible for this in your department?

Conclude:

★ We can see that many serious production problems can
★ arise by not having everything ready for instruction.

(b) Have the Workplace properly arranged.

Ask questions—get brief discussion.

★ Why should it be properly arranged?

★ What effect may this have on Safety?

★ In your plant, is this a part of standard procedure?

★ If this is poorly done, what problems may arise?

(2) Prepare Yourself

★ When this is not done or done ineffectively the situation
★ can lead to serious production problems.

★ What are some of the ways you can prepare yourself for
★ job instruction?

Put answers on board. Brief discussion.

Questions:

★ Why should you prepare yourself for job instruction?

★ Is this standard procedure in your plant?

★ Name a few problems that can arise if you do not prepare
★ yourself.

★ The most important preparation step is to breakdown the
★ job for instruction purposes, separating the job into Impor-
★ tant Steps, together with the Key Points in each step.

★ Another preparation step is to decide in what order you
★ will instruct the job, and if it should be broken up into
★ smaller instructional units for ease and effectiveness.

Questions:

★ Why is "Order of Instruction" important?

★ Could this lead to a production problem?

★ When should this decision be made?

★ Acquaint yourself with the hazards of the job as well as
★ strange terms and trade names.

★ How could this lead to a production problem?

★ The lack of clearly organizing the job in one's mind is the
★ principal reason for poor or faulty instruction, resulting in
★ the following:

Scrap, Rework, Accidents, Delays, Mistakes, Broken tools, Damaged equipment, Spoiled materials, Low productivity, Discouraged workers, etc.

JOB INSTRUCTION SHEET

★ We will now present the Job Instruction Sheet and how
★ to make one.

Hand out sample Job Instruction sheets. Use chart for discussion.

BREAKDOWN THE JOB

- *Why is it necessary?*
  To <u>clearly organize the job</u> in one's mind.

- *What is its purpose?*
  To <u>know what you are going to instruct; how much;</u> and <u>in what order</u>.

- *Where should it be done?*
  Right on the job.

- *When should it be done?*
  Every time you hae any instructing to do. (Once completed, file for future use.)

- *Who should do it?*
  The person who is to do the instructing. Supervisor—Foreman—lead person, etc.

- *How is the best way to make a job breakdown?*
  Here is a quick, simple way to do it:

	JOB BREAKDOWN SHEET FOR TRAINING MAN ON NEW JOB	
Operation: SET UP TO DRILL #1 HOLE		Part: DRILL PRESS #55
IMPORTANT STEPS IN THE OPERATION		**KEY POINTS**
Step: A logical segment of the operation when something happens to ADVANCE the work.		Key Point: Anything in a shop that might — Make or break the job. Make the work easier to do, i.e., bit of special information.
1	GET SPECIFICATION SHEET AND TOOLS FOR THE JOB	FROM TOOL CRIB CHECK TOOLS WITH SPECS
2	SET MACHINE SPEED	ADJUST BELTS AN DPULLEYS
3	SET UP MACHINE	INSERT PROPER DRILL AND TIGHTEN ADJUST TO HEIGH AND SET STOPS
4	INSTRUCT THE OPERATOR	FOLLOW JOB INSTRUCTION SHEET USE JOB INSTRUCTION TECHNIQUES
5	GAGE FIRST FEW PIECES	USE PLUG GATE #3654

Annotations to the left of the breakdown sheet:

*1. The first thing you do is to fill in the headings.—▶

*2. Next you list the —▶

Start doing the job until there is—▶

Then write it in this space as step—▶

Continue the job, listing the important steps in the consecutive spaces.

*3. Start doing the job again. Do the first step . Pick out the Key Points.

List them briefly opposite Step 1. in the proper space. ontinue with the job, doing each step, picking out the key points,

* <u>Breakdowns</u> are <u>not</u> micro-motion studies, job descriptions, nor instruction sheets for workers. They are just simple, common-sense outlines that you make of the job, so you will not overlook or miss anything when you instruct another on that job.

★ Often while preparing a Job Instruction Sheet one may
★ come upon the answer to his production problems.

★ To breakdown a job for instruction, it is important that we
★ understand the two principal parts involved: (chart)

IMPORTANT STEPS

KEY POINTS

★ Important Step: (What is done?)

As the job is done, observe closely for the parts of the operation when something is done to advance the job. Question what is being done.

These steps should include inspections and automatic machine operations, in their proper sequence.
A step is not every conceivable action or motion.

★ Key Point: (How it is done?)

Nearly every Important Step has a certain exact and definite way in which it must be done. These are the keys to the way the job must be performed, and so are called KEY POINTS.

If the step is done as the Key Points state, then it will be performed correctly and little or no trouble should be experienced.

If the Key Points are omitted or not explained fully in the instruction, then expect to have the following troubles:

    Poor quality and quantity of work
    Accidents
    Low productivity
    Discouraged workers
    Wasted materials and supplies
    Broken tools and equipment
    etc.

★ Many Key Points are more or less obvious, but if in
★ doubt, then:

Probe for the Key Points. Ask questions as the job is done:
    "What would happen if......?
    "What difference does it make if......?
    "Why did you......?

Prove the Key Points. Question the answers to the above with:
    Does it make or break the job?
    Will it injure the worker? (Safety is always a key
                    point.)
    Will it make the job easier to do?

(3) Prepare the Learner

★ Questions: (Discuss briefly)

Why should we prepare the learner?

Is this a standard procedure in your plant?

How should we prepare the learner?

Present: (Board or Chart)

Put at ease
Find out what he knows about the job
Interest him in learning the job
Position him correctly for instruction

Point out that:

Preparing the learner for instruction, correctly and fully is a good way to prevent many production problems.

---

25 min **PROBLEMS IN PERSONALITY SITUATION**

When the problem is PEOPLE who: _____

Don't Care
Won't Do
---

then we have a personality situation which involves Attitude and Behavior.

What are some problems resulting from personality situations?

Put answers on board—Brief discussion.

Questions:

★ Are these types of problems common in your plant?

★ Tell me about your experience with such problems.

★ In preparing for solution of such problems, what would you
★ do?

Present this part of Step 2. (board or by chart)

Get the Facts   —   Weigh the Facts   —   Make the Discussion

★ Which of these is the most important? Why?

★ What do you understand by the term "Fact"?

★ How do you get Facts? Brief Discussion.

Present, "Get the Facts."   (board or chart)

Review the records
What rules and plant customs apply
Talk with individuals concerned
Get opinions and feelings

Questions:

★ What records would you review?

★ What are you searching after?

★ Where will you find such records?

★ Why are records considered good facts?

★ Why should rules and plant customs be considered?

★ Where will you learn of these in your search for facts?

"Talk with individuals concerned."

Questions: (Get brief discussion on each)

★ Who will you talk with?

★ Where will you find these individuals?

★ What will you talk about?

You are attempting to "Get their Opinions and Feelings."

★ Should opinions and feelings be considered as facts?

★ How do you get opinions and feelings?

Present:
        Don't argue
        Encourage him to talk about what seems important to
            him
        Don't interrupt
        Don't jump to conclusions
        Don't do all the talking yourself
        Listen

Conclude:

Before any problem can be solved you must get the facts, for upon them is based the answer or correction. Be sure you have the whole story.

In preparing to correct PEOPLE problems dealing with personality situations, getting the facts is most important.

Present, "Weigh the Facts."

After the facts are gathered they must be considered from these points"

Do they fit together?
Are there any gaps, omissions or contradictions?
Consider their bearing upon each other
Check against company policies and practices

Present, "Make the Decision."

We are now ready to make a decision in the preparing for solution of the PEOPLE problem:

Make final analysis of the facts
What possible action can be taken?
Weigh the consequences
Question the psychological effect
Leave a way open for him to "save face"
Consider the effect upon the individual, group and company
Decide on the final action
Don't jump to conclusions

1 hr
to here

---

50 min **PRACTICE DEMONSTRATIONS**

★ We will now have some practice demonstrations in
★ PEOPLE Problems.

The first one will be a case where the person "Didn't Know" or "Couldn't Do," resulting in faulty instruction.

Have the member come to the head of the table.
Explain what he is to do.

★ Please tell your problem.

★ How do you know you have a problem?

Have him explain his Step 1, "Isolate the Problem" to the group. (Brief discussion—get agreement)

Have him tell how he would "Get Ready to Instruct."

★ How would you prepare the work place?
(get brief discussion and agreement)

If appropriate use the board to sketch work place.

★ How would you prepare yourself?

Have him explain his Job Instruction Sheet.
Fill in breakdown on large Breakdown Sheet.
(get brief discussion and agreement)

★ How would you prepare the learner?
(get brief discussion and agreement)

Demonstrate this point with another group member.

Thank the member and have him return to his seat.

★ We will now apply the things WE have learned in consider-
★ ing "People Problems" which concern ATTITUDE and
★ BEHAVIOR.

★ I will tell a Problem and together we will apply Step 2,
★ using worksheet.

Pass out a copy of, "Outline for Handling Problem."
Draw FACTS from the group.
Question according to the pattern placed on the board earlier
in this Session.
For practice in WEIGH the FACTS use the questions on the
board as above.
The details outlined under MAKE THE DECISION on a previous
Manual page to be used as a guide.

★ The second practice demonstration will be a case where
★ the person "Didn't Care" or "Wouldn't Do," resulting in
★ an Attitude or Behavior Problem.

Have member come to head of table.

★ Please tell your problem.

44

★ How do you know you have a problem?

Have him explain his Step 1, "Isolate the Problem" to the group. (Brief discussion—get agreement)

To group:

★ How do we prepare to solve this problem?

★ Tell us the facts as you know them (place on board).

★ Should we let the group ask questions?

    Add only those facts to which the "Supervisor" agrees.

★ What do we do next? (Answer—Weigh the Facts)

Have group participate in weighing the facts.

★ Are we now ready to make a decision?

★ How do we do this? Why?

★ What do we consider? Why?
    (get brief discussion and agreement)

★ Have we prepared this problem for solution?

Thank member and have him return to his seat.

CONCLUSION OF STEP 2

In this step we have presented the technique of "Preparing for Solution."

This is preparatory to the next step and covers the whole problem possibilities in industry.

Review:

When the problem is MECHANICAL involving such things as:

    Methods, Tools, Layout, Machines, Equipment, Materials, etc.

We learned that a Flow Chart is useful to look at the whole problem.

The Flow Diagram is often used when layout seems to be the problem.

When we discovered that the problem was in a specific place or job we learned that we should break it down into details and question every detail. Here is where we are most likely to find the trouble.

When the problem is PEOPLE who "Don't Know" or "Can't Do," then we learned that it is due to faulty instruction, so we must prepare for job instruction if we are to correct such situations.

We learned that we first must "Get Ready" by having the proper tools, etc. and having them properly arranged.

Next we learned that the most important tool for "Getting Yourself Ready to Instruct" is to breakdown the operation for instructional purposes. Here we list the Important Steps in the operation and list the Key Points of each step. These are the keys to the job.

Then in PEOPLE problems who, "Don't Care" or "Won't Do" we have a personality situation dealing with attitude and behavior. It is here that most human relation problems are found. We learn how to prepare for their solution by:

> Getting all the facts.
> Weighing these facts.
> Making the decision.

ASSIGNMENTS FOR SESSION V

We will want practice problems at the next session in MECHANICAL and PEOPLE problems.

We will use the same problems that were used in Sessions III and IV, as we will want to carry them on to corrections in Session V.

Have Step 1 fully completed on these problems.

BEFORE THE SESSION STARTS

Be there 15 minutes before the session starts.

Have everything ready:

      Chairs, tables, blackboard, etc,

      Hand-outs for Step 3 and Step 4. (1 per member)

      Charts for Step 1, Step 2, Step 3, and Step 4.

OPEN SESSION V

Greet members cordially.

Review:

Step 1—ISOLATE THE PROBLEM (chart)
      Stress its importance. (brief discussion)

Step 2—PREPARE FOR SOLUTION (chart)
      Stress the three parts of the step.
      Tell of the importance of Step 2.

★ Let me again state that this program is designed to help
★ Supervisors solve their day to day production problems.

★ It is developed primarily for use at the department or the
★ division level.

★ We know that all Supervisors have problems.
★ It is these problems that interfere with his ability to get out
★ production of good quality, on time, with safety.

★ We have learned how to Isolate these problems, and how
★ to Prepare for their Solution, and now we are ready to
★ continue further with the problem solving pattern.

3 min
to here

---

5 min ## STEP 3 HEADINGS

★ We will now present Step 3.

Develop Step 3 headings from group—place on board.

★ We are now ready to "CORRECT THE PROBLEM" (Step 3).
    (board or chart)

Present Step 3. Hand out Step 3. (board or chart)

★ In this step we carry on the two parts as we did in Step 2.

MECHANICAL PROBLEMS
PEOPLE PROBLEMS

8 min
to here

Explain briefly. Get discussion and agreement.

DEVELOP THE NEW METHOD

★ For simplicity in learning the problem solving pattern we
★ will again take up the MECHANICAL problems first.
★ Problems involving Methods, Layout, Tools, Equipment,
★ Machines, Materials, etc.

Present: "Develop the New Method"   (board or chart)

Explain:
This step is actually a reasoning process.
We use the answers to the questions asked in Step 2 together with the ideas and notes we jotted down on the Breakdown Sheet to finally arrive at an improvement, or correction, of the problem.

We can make improvements or correct "mechanical" problems when details are:

ELIMINATED
COMBINED
REARRANGED
SIMPLIFIED

Show relationship between the questions asked in Step 2 and Develop a New Method, in Step 3. (Chart)

Eliminate Unnecessary Details:

We eliminate details to solve the problems when it is due to:
    Unnecessary use of manpower—machines—tools — materials—time.

Questions:

★ How can you tell if a detail is unnecessary?

★ Who is best qualified to answer the question in your
★ department?

Point out that:
    Many production problems arise here.

Combine details in whole or in part where practical:

★ We combine details when the problem is:
    Transportations—Inspections—Delays—Storages.

★ When the problem involves the place—time—person,
★ we consider combining details where practical.

Questions:

★ When would this be impractical?

★ Who determines the best place—time—person to do
★ a job in your company?

> Point out that:
>   Many production problems start here.

Rearrange Details for Better Sequence Where Practical:

★ We rearrange details when the problem is one of location
★ or excessive handlings—backtracking—delays—
★ accident hazards—maintenance possibilities—
★ working conditions.

Questions:

★ Why would this be impractical at times?

★ How would such problems be discovered?

★ How would you proceed to have details rearranged in
★ sequence in your department?

> Point out that:
>   Many production problems can be corrected in this
>   way.

Simplify all Necessary Details:

★ We simplify all necessary details when the problem is to:

    Reduce non-productive work motions.

    Make the work easier and safer to do.

★ This is done only after we have tried to correct the
★ problem by:

    Eliminating unnecessary details.

    Combining or Rearranging details where practical.

★ In simplifying jobs when solving production problems we
★ often find that the answer is in:

    Pre-positioning of Material, Tools, Gauges, etc., in the
    best place in the proper work area.

    Using gravity feed hoppers if practical

    Using drop delivery chutes if practical.

51

Letting both hands do useful work.

Using jigs and fixtures instead of hands to hold work.

RECORD PROPOSED CORRECTION

We are now ready to complete the breakdown sheet by recording the proposed correction in the right hand column.

Work with same group member whose problem was used in Session III.
Complete the breakdown.

Point out that:
    There are usually less details in the proposed correction. (Get brief discussion and agreement)

PUT THE CORRECTION INTO EFFECT

★ We are now ready to make the correction.

★ We will follow the proposed correction on the breakdown
★ sheet.

★ Get approval of all concerned:

    How soon will you do this?

    Who do you need to help you on this?

    Who will you contact to secure approval?

    Why is it necessary to consult others?

    Who actually will put the correction into effect?

PRACTICE STEP 3—MECHANICAL PROBLEMS

★ We will now practice Step 3 of the MECHANICAL
★ problem solving pattern.

Have member come to the head of the table with his breakdown.

Have him place the "Present Method" on the board. Members copy same on blank breakdown sheet.

★ Now please show the group how you have arrived at the
★ correction of your problem.

> Have him go through the questioning process, making notes
> and listing ideas.
>
> Have him develop the new or corrected method and place on
> the board in right hand column of breakdown sheet.

★ Now, can we let the group ask questions?
> (Get permission of member)

Get brief discussion from members.

Conclude:

★ This practice, though brief, shows us how to correct
★ MECHANICAL production problems.

★ We will have more practice later.

> Thank member for his interest and cooperation and have him
> return to his seat.

INSTRUCT THE LEARNER

★ We have presented the pattern to use in correcting prod-
★ uction problems when the cause is MECHANICAL such as:
★ Methods, Layout, Tools, Equipment, Machines, Material, etc.

★ Now we will consider the production problems which
★ predominantly involve PEOPLE.

All production problems involve people either directly or indirectly. We have divided the PEOPLE problems section into two
categories.

1. Problems due to faulty instruction.
2. Problems due to personality situation and job
assignment.

★ Let us first present the correction of production problems
★ due to faulty instruction and its preparation.

★ We learned in Step 2 how to Get Ready to Instruct, which
★ briefly is:

Prepare the Workplace   (use board or chart)
Prepare Yourself
Prepare the Learner

★ Now we will continue with the problem solving pattern
★ for problems involving PEOPLE who, "Don't Know" or
★ "Can't Do."

★ These problems account for a high percent of all produc-
★ tion problems, which result in: Scrap, Rework, Delays,
★ Accidents, Damaged tools and equipment, Spoilage of
★ Materials, Low productivity, etc.

★ In Step 2 we prepared the learner for instruction. Now to
★ correct faulty instruction problems we will use this pattern:

Place on board or use chart.

INSTRUCT

TRY-OUT

PUT ON HIS OWN

★ Experience has shown that the following method of instruc-
★ ting a worker is best, and its consistent use will prevent
★ many of the common day to day production problems that
★ a Supervisor has.

Questions:

★ Who has had problems due to faulty instruction?

★ Whose responsibility is it to instruct in your plant?

★ What problems can result from faulty instruction?

★ We are now ready to present the three steps of instructing:
    (chart)

★ INSTRUCT

> TELL what you are SHOWING (Use illustrations when
>   necessary).
> One Important Step at a time, following the job instruc-
>   tion sheet.
> Stress the KEY POINTS in each step giving their impor-
>   tance.
> Repeat as often as necessary, testing him with "W"
>   questions.

★ TRY-OUT THE LEARNER'S PERFORMANCE

> Have him do the job. Correct his errors at once.
> Have him repeat TELLING what he is SHOWING,
>   stressing the KEY POINTS giving their importance.
> Test him with "WHY" questions.

★ <u>PUT HIM ON HIS OWN</u>
    Stress quality and safety.
    Encourage questions about the job.
    Tell him who to ask for help.
    Leave him on his own.

★ A great many production problems can be corrected by
★ the use of this simple instruction technique. It is easy to
★ use and very effective.

Questions:

    How would correct instruction methods prevent production problems?

    Why follow the Job Instruction sheet while instructing?

    What is the purpose of using "W" questions while instructing?

    Who is responsible for instructing workers in your plant?

PRACTICE DEMONSTRATION

Use the problem for which the Job Instruction sheet was made in Step 3.

Place large Job Instruction sheet on wall or copy on board.
Leader do the instruction or have a group member do it.
Select a group member for a "learner."
Review the "Get Ready to Instruct Points."
Teach the job using the above standardized pattern.
Do a perfect job of instructing as a pattern for following demonstrations.
Thank member for his cooperation.

★ This demonstration of instruction as a method of correction
★ of production problems due to faulty instruction was brief
★ but we will have more practice later.

TAKE ACTION

★ A great many of the Supervisor's day to day problems are
★ personality situations type or cases where PEOPLE
★ "Don't Care" or "Won't Do."

★ There are always problems in attitudes and behavior and
★ they require quick and careful solution.

★ In Session IV, Step 2, we learned that we must "Get the
★ Facts," then weigh them to see if we had the whole story,
★ then arrive at a decision.

★ We are now ready in Step 3, "Correct the Problem," to
★ TAKE ACTION.

★ There are some important things to remember before
★ taking your action:

> Consider the best time and place to do it.
> Explain the action to the person; Why it is best for him.
> Give advantages and benefits to him.. Get acceptance.
> Are you going to handle this yourself?

★ Put the action or decision into effect.
★ Consider feelings and attitudes.

★ Secure understanding.

★ Notify all concerned.

Questions:

★ Why should you consider time and place before taking
★ action?

★ Why do you think it well to explain the action fully and
★ get his acceptance?

★ Who "takes action" in such cases in your plant?

PRACTICE DEMONSTRATION

★ We will now have a demonstration of a problem where a
★ personality situation exists.
★ We will continue with the same problem that was prepared
★ for solution in Session IV, Step 2.

> Have the member come to the head of the table.

★ State the problem again to refresh our memory.
★ Review just what was done in Step 2 on this problem.

> Place "Action" on the board. Members copy same on their
> forms. (Brief discussion)

★ This demonstration was brief but we will have more
★ practice later.

Thank the member and have him return to his seat.

CHECK AND EVALUATE THE RESULTS

★ We have learned how to:

ISOLATE THE PROBLEM   STEP 1   (chart)
PREPARE FOR SOLUTION   STEP 2   (chart)
MAKE THE CORRECTION   STEP 3   (chart)

★ Now that the correction of the problem has been made
★ we must:

CHECK AND EVALUATE THE RESULTS   STEP 4 (chart or board)

> Pass out Step 4 sheet.

The checking and evaluating of results of correcting a production problem may be done in various ways, depending upon the conditions present in the company together with their practices and policies.

Here is how to Check and Evaluate the Results of the correction:

1. Check as soon as possible or practicable to learn if the correction has been made.

2. Keep alert of the Human Angle because where changes have been made people often build up a Resistance or a Resentment to it. Such feelings will present itself in various:

Attitudes—Behaviors—Relationship situations.

3. Keep a close check on the situation to detect any signs of a new problem being created by this correction. People often react to changes as threats to their basic job wants, such as:

Recognition—Security—Job Satisfaction.

4. Evaluate the results by consulting records where available:

Production records
Quality records
Accident records
Productivity records
Attendance records
Grievance records
Cost records

Note the results of these records and inform all concerned of progress and results.

5. Look for ways to prevent a recurrence of the problem.

★ "Did your action help production?"

PROBLEM SOLVING PRACTICE ASSIGNMENTS

★ We have completed the 4-step problem solving pattern
★ and are now ready for practice in its use to increase our
★ proficiency in solving the day to day production problems
★ we meet in business and industry.

> Pass out the "Master Sheet" of the program.
> Display the chart of the complete program.
> Briefly review and discuss the overall pattern, pointing out the relationship of the three basic programs of Supervision and their use in solving problems.

★ This 4-step pattern is rather extensive but complete. It is
★ designed for help in solving any production problem at the
★ department or division level in a practical way. It is also
★ applicable to most any level of Supervision and to other
★ forms of business.

★ Many of the daily problems in industry will not need the
★ application of the entire pattern. Only those parts that
★ apply should be used.

Assignments:

Each one is to bring in a production problem completely solved with all necessary details and facts pertaining to it, ready for presentation to the group.

All forms necessary for its proper solution must also be presented:

Step 1 "Isolate the Problem" form
Flow Chart
Flow Diagram
Methods Breakdown
Job Instruction Sheet

Where the problem is due to faulty instruction, bring in the sample problem. Where the problem is an attitude or behavior situation, be prepared with all facts and information about the problem for proper presentation.

So that we may have a variety of problems for practice, each member will be assigned a certain type of problem. All members of the group will have an opportunity to participate in the discussions.

★ I will visit the various plants with you to help select the
★ problems.

<u>Session VI</u>	Mechanical problem
	Faulty Instruction problem
	Attitude or Behavioral problem
<u>Session VII</u>	Mechanical problem
	Faulty Instruction problem
	Attitude or Behavioral problem
<u>Session VIII</u>	Mechanical problem
	Faulty Instruction problem
	Attitude or Behavioral problem
	Mixed problem

*2 hr
to here*

SESSION VI—REVIEW THE 4 STEPS

Stress the importance of using the 4-step problem solving plan for correcting production problems.

Review the 4 steps. (Refer to the Master pattern sheet, or chart)

★ Why is it important to Isolate the Problem?

★ How do you Isolate a Problem? (Use Step 1 sheet, or chart)

★ Why are Steps 2 and 3 separated into three sections? (Use chart)

5 min
to here   ★ Tell the value of Step 4.

---

40 min   ## PRACTICE DEMONSTRATION

Value of Demonstrations

Gain confidence by doing what we have learned.
We see practical application of these principles in our own jobs.
Everyone of us has the same opportunity to show his ability in the use of the problem solving plan.

We will have three demonstrations in this session.

1st — The Mechanical problem		40 Min.
2nd— The Faulty Instruction problem		35 Min.
3rd — The Attitude and Behavior problem		35 Min.

Have member come to head of the table, bringing his material.

Pass out blank forms of Step 1 and Step 2 to members.

Demonstration procedure for presenting the Mechanical problem.

1. Describe the problem (Tell in a natural narrative manner).
   What is the problem?
   Who is affected?
   What are the effects of the problem?
   When and where did it start?

2. Explain how the problem was isolated.

   Use large chart or board. Members to copy data on their sheets.

61

3. Explain how Step 2 was used to analyze the overall situation.

> Use large Flow Chart or board showing present method. (Members copy)

> Use Flow Diagram if needed to show overall layout. (Copy on board)

4. Explain how Step 2 was used to analyze the specific situation.

> Use large Job Methods Breakdown chart, or board showing present method. Members copy.

> Use the questioning method to demonstrate how facts were discovered, which enable you to develop a new method, thus correcting the problem (Members do not participate at this time).

5. Explain how Step 3 was used in developing a new method or in making a correction to the problem.

If Flow Chart or Flow Diagram furnished sufficient facts to make the "correction" then:

> Use large Flow Chart showing the proposed situation. (Members copy)

> Use the Flow Diagram (board) showing the proposed layout.

If analysis of the specific situation was needed to make the correction then:

> Complete the Methods Breakdown using chart or board showing the proposed or corrected method. Members copy.

6. Explain how Step 4 will be used in this problem.
    When and Where will the correction be made?
    Who will be notified of the correction?
    What facts and data will be collected to prove the problem is solved.
    Could this problem have been prevented? How?

★ We will now have questions about how the problem solving
★ pattern was used in this demonstration.

Have members ask questions. All answers are referred to the "Supervisor" who made the presentation. "It is his problem."

If further improvements or corrections can be made it demonstrates that problems need all of the facts before a final answer can be given, or that corrections may be made in more than one manner.

Use remaining time, if any, to review how the problem was isolated, and how it was prepared for solution, and finally how it was corrected.

Thank member and have him return to his seat.

35 min **PRACTICE DEMONSTRATION**

★ We will now have a demonstration of how to correct a
★ problem due to faulty instruction.
  (Members refer to Master Chart)

Have Member come to head of table with his Material.
Solicit another Member to be the "learner."
Pass out blank Job Instruction sheets.

Procedure for Presenting "Faulty Instruction" Problem
Get Ready to Instruct

1. Explain how the work place was prepared.
    State the job setting. Tools, Machines, Materials, etc.
    Sketch the job layout (Simple sketch on board)

2. Explain how to prepare yourself.
    Draw outline of Job Instruction sheet on board
    Fill in Important Steps and Key Points in their proper spaces. (Members copy)

3. Explain the order of instruction to be used.

4. Demonstrate how the learner is prepared.

    Have learner approach the work place.

    Put the learner at ease.
    State the Job. Learn his experience.
    Interest him in learning the job.
    State the use and case of tools, equipment, gauges, safeguards, etc.
    Place him in correct position for learning.

Instruct the Learner

5. Demonstrate the regular step by step method of instruction.
    Instruct
    Tryout his performance
    Put him on his own

★ We will now have questions about how the Problem
★ Solving pattern was used in this demonstration.

Have Members ask questions and comment on demonstration. All answer as referred to the "Supervisor" who made the demonstration.
    "It is his problem."

Use remaining time, if any, to review how the problem was solved by correct instruction.

Thank members and have them return to their seats.

---

35 min **PRACTICE DEMONSTRATION**

★ We will now conclude the practice demonstrations for this
★ session by observing how one of our members handled a
★ problem involving Attitude and Behavior.

Have member come to head of table with his notes and material.

Pass out Step 1 worksheets.
Pass out Job Relations worksheets.
Ask members to fill out worksheet from the information of the demonstration.

Procedure for presenting an Attitude and Behavior Problem

1. Tell the incident or situation that caused you to realize that you had a problem.

2. Tell which one of the following ways from which this problem arose.

   (a) Did you sense a change in your department?
   (b) Did you anticipate a change in your department?
   (c) Did this problem come to you?
   (d) Did you run into this problem?

The purpose of bringing out how problems arise is to make you realize how preventive work may be done, particularly in regard to (a) and (b) above.

3. Explain how the problem was isolated. Step 1.

Use large chart or board. Members copy same on their sheets.

Go through each sub-head of Step 1 and tell how it was used and how it applies to this problem.

4. Explain how you prepared for the solution of this problem. Step 2.

Go through each sub-head of Step 2 and tell how it was used in preparing for the solution of this problem.

Get the Facts

   Write the facts of this case on the board.
      (Members copy)

   Tell what records were reviewed.

Tell what rules and regulations were consulted.
Tell which persons were consulted for opinions and feelings.

Weigh the Facts

Tell how the facts fit together. Show their relationship.
Show that there are no contradictions or gaps that calls for additional facts.
Show how you considered their bearing upon each other.

Table Make a Decision

List the possible actions that could be reasonably made.
   (Members copy)

Tell how you considered the effect of this decision upon the individual, the group, and on production.
   (Members copy)

Tell what the final decision is and give reasons for its selection.

5. Explain how Step 3 will be used.

Go through each sub-head, explain how used. Refer to chart.

Take Action

Tell how you considered time and place for the action and why you selected these.

Tell what was used to explain the benefits and advantages of this action to the individual.

Explain exactly how the action will be put into effect.

Tell how you will get understanding and acceptance of the decision.

6. Explain how Step 4 will be used. Follow master outline for problem solving sheet or chart.

When and where will the correction or action be made?

Who will be notified?

What records will be consulted to evaluate the results of this corrective action?

★ Could this problem have been prevented?
   (Have group discussion)

★ In considering the Human Angle, what changes in Attitude
★ and Behavior would you look for?

Thank member and have him return to his seat.

---

5 min   Review of Session VI.

Make assignments for next session.

2 hrs   Close session.
to here

SESSION VII—PRACTICE DEMONSTRATIONS

Time
Table
5 min

★ In the last session we had practice in solving production
★ problems dealing with MECHANICAL situations and with
★ PEOPLE situations.

> Review the 4-step master pattern.
> (Refer to hand-out and chart)

5 min
to here

---

1 hr
55 min

★ We will continue with practice demonstrations to increase
★ our skill in the use of the 4-step pattern for solving produc-
★ tion problems which we experience daily at the depart-
★ ment level in industry.

1st demonstration — Mechanical problem.	40 Min.
2nd demonstration — Faulty Instruction problem.	40 Min.
3rd demonstration — Attitude and Behavior problem.	35 Min.

> Follow the same procedure for the demonstrations as we used
> in Session VI.

★ In our next and last session we will continue with practice
★ demonstrations.

★ The assignments will be somewhat different and will
★ include what we call "Mixed situations" problems such as:

(a) A Mechanical problem combined with a Faulty instruction problem.

(b) A Faulty instruction problem combined with a problem involving Attitude and Behavior.

2 hrs
to here

SESSION VIII—PRACTICE DEMONSTRATIONS

★ This is the final session in the program and we will contin-
★ ue to practice so as to improve our skill in solving produc-
★ tion problems.

1st demonstration — "Mechanical" problem.   35 Min.
2nd demonstration— "Mechanical" and a "Faulty Instruction"
                                 combined problem.
                                             40 Min.
3rd demonstration —"Faulty Instruction" and an "Attitude
                                and Behavior" combined problem.
                                           35 Min.

> Follow the same procedure as before for each of the three dem-
> onstrations.

APPLYING THE PROBLEM SOLVING PATTERN

★ We have arrived at the end of this program for solving
★ production problems.
★ At the opening of the program we discussed the Duties and
★ Responsibilities of the Supervisor.
    (Refer to the "hand-out")

★ You have learned the entire pattern for solving day to day
★ problems and have had practice in using it. Now you will
★ soon be able to practice the skill which you received here
★ in your own industry, in your own department.
    (Write the 4-steps on board, or use chart.)

> Restate the urgent need for:
>
> | Full | PRODUCTION |
> |------|------------|
> | of good | QUALITY |
> | on | SCHEDULE |
> | at | LOW COST |
> | with | SAFETY |

★ Although we can foresee many problems at their inception
★ and can prevent them from arising, it is quite improbable
★ that all problems can be forseen or prevented.

★ It has been said that one of the principal Duties and Respo-
★ nsibilities of a Supervisor is to keep a smooth running
★ department.

★ This is what all Supervisors strive for but never quite attain.

★ So long as we are dealing with PEOPLE we will have
★ problems.

★ These problems can be solved by fully and conscientiously
★ applying this 4-step pattern. It will work if used properly
★ and regularly.

★ Emphasize that the only sure way that a Supervisor can get
★ a smooth running department is to follow this 4-step pat-
★ tern of problem solving, otherwise he is only a "trouble
★ shooter" dealing with one emergency after another and
★ never quite getting them solved.

★ Many Supervisors will say that they don't have time to use
★ such a pattern for solving problems, but experience shows
★ that they will use much more time "shooting trouble" and
★ never get the problem solved.

★ Just what are you going to do about this?

Point out:

> Use the 4 -step pattern for solving all of your problems.
> Make it a habit.
> Use it fully.
> Have the various forms which were used in the program,
>> prepared especially to fit your own plant and
>> department.
> Solving problems is your responsibility as a Supervisor.

★ Thank you for your attention, interest and cooperation in
★ this program.

★ I wish you success.

Adjourn the session.

DUTIES AND RESPONSIBILITIES OF A SUPERVISORY PERSON

To coordinate with the remainder of the Organization.

To operate in accordance with company policies.
To operate according to schedule and specifications.
To cooperate with staff and other departments.
To keep management informed at all times.

To make effective use of Manpower.

To place the right man on the right job.
To start the new employee.
To train the employee for jobs which are new to him.
To improve job performance of each person.
To gain cooperation and develop smooth working
    relationships.
To interpret company policies.
To control labor costs.
To protect potential abilities of each person.
To create and maintain high department morale.

To make effective use of Materials and Equipment.

To plan for efficient handling and storing of equipment.
To control material costs.
To control machinery and equipment costs.
To maintain safe operating conditions.

SOLVING PROBLEMS

Does this problem involve: THINGS? ☐   PLACES? ☐   PEOPLE? ☐

Exactly what is the problem?

Does this problem concern: QUALITY? ◯   QUANTITY? ◯   SAFETY? ◯   COST? ◯

What is the proof or evidence of the problem?

What caused the problem?

What would you do about this?

Date:_____ Dept:_____Name:_____

AN OUTLINE FOR SOLVING PROBLEMS

What is the problem?

List possible causes	List possible corrections

Exactly what should be done about it?	When?	Who do you need to help?

ALL JOBS CONSIST OF THESE PARTS

Movement of material without definite work accomplishment is either:

        Make ready
        Put away
        Waste

Eliminate every step that does not contribute to the end result.

MAKE READY	
This is the time and effort spent in getting things ready, such as: Materials, Tools, Equipment, and Gauges. Also the placing of the material or part in the nearby work area, from trucks, pans, racks, etc.	
	**DO** This is the work that actually accomplishes the desired main objective and does add to the value of it. e.g. Drill a hole, Plane a board, etc.
PUT AWAY This includes all details necessary to complete the job after the "DO" operation. It includes setting the part aside and/or placing on trucks, in pans, on racks, on conveyors, etc.	

The greatest opportunity for improvement is in "MAKE READY" and "PUT AWAY."
They add to the time and cost, but not to the value of the product.

Less than 50% of the total time is consumed by the "DO" part of the job.
The "MAKE READY" and "PUT AWAY" should be cleaned up after first attempting to improve the "DO" details.

TRAINING TIMETABLE SAMPLES

TRAINING TIMETABLE (SAMPLE)

BRANCH: <u>PRODUCTION</u>
UNIT: <u>SHEET METAL FACTORY NO. 1</u>

Supervisor: <u>Higashi, Foreman, Factory 1</u>
Reviewed by: <u>Kuroda, Factory Chief</u>
Date Reviewed: <u>5 Jan. '09</u>

Simple Operations → ← Longer Operations

JOBS OR OPERATIONS →

NAMES	Job No.	Develop 1	Shears 2	Hammer 3	Roll 4	Planish 5	Bend 6	File 7	Press 8	Die 9	Heat treat 10	Solder 11	Weld 12	Rivet 13	Assemble 14	Refine 15	16	REMARKS
1 Mr. Adachi		v	v	v	v	v	v	v	v	v	v	v	v	v	v	v		
2 Mr. Banjo		v	v	v	v	1-12	1-15	v	v	v	v	v	v	v	v			
3 Mr. Chiba		v	v	v	1-12	1-20	1-25	v	v	v	v	2-5	v	v	v			
4 Mr. Daimaru		1-15	1-22	1-31	2-5	2-20	2-25	3-5	3-10	–	–	3-15	–	3-20	3-25	3-31		
5 Mr. Endo		1-20	1-31	2-10	2-15	2-28	3-5	–	3-15	–	–	–	–	–	3-31			
6 Mr. Fuchida		1-20	1-31	2-10	2-15	2-28	3-5	3-15	–	–	–	3-25	–	–	4-5			
7																		
8																		

v = Adequately trained
2-10 = Date Training is to be completed
– = Not Required to know this job

TRAINING TIMETABLE (SAMPLE)

BRANCH: _____
UNIT: _____

Supervisor: _____
Reviewed by: _____
Date Reviewed: _____

Simple Operations → ← Longer Operations

JOBS OR OPERATIONS →

NAMES	Job No.	1	2	3	4	5	6	7	8	9	10	11	12	13	14	15	16	REMARKS
1																		
2																		
3																		
4																		
5																		
6																		
7																		
8																		

= Adequately trained
= Date Training is to be completed
= Not Required to know this job

HOW TO SOLVE PRODUCTION PROBLEMS

STEP 1—ISOLATE THE PROBLEM

1. State the Problem:	Is it Mechanical, pertaining to things and pieces? Is it People who: Don't Know, Can't Do, Don't Care, Won't Do?
2. Prove the Problem:	Statistical data of trouble in production, performance attitude.
3. Explore the Cause:	Is it Methods, Layout, Tools, Equipment, Materials, Design, or Hazards? Is it Wrong assignment? Faulty Instruction? Personality situation?
4. Draw Conclusions:	Is it MECHANICAL? PEOPLE? or BOTH?

STEP 2—PREPARE FOR SOLUTION

Is it MECHANICAL?	Is it ... PEOPLE?	who ...
Methods, Layout, Materials, Tools, Equipment, Design.	Don't Know? Can't Do?	Don't Care? Won't Do?
then improve... Method for Better Way	then improve... Knowledge—Productivity—Skill	then improve... Attitude and Behavior

ANALYZE:
 (1) Overall situation
     (1) Flow Chart
     (2) Flow Diagram
     Question overall job
 (2) Specific situation
     (1) Method
     (2) Method breakdown
     (3) Layout
     (4) Work situation set-up
 	
 QUESTION EACH DETAIL
 Using questions starting with:
 WHY?, WHAT?, WHERE?,
 WHEN?, WHO?, HOW?
	GET READY TO INSTRUCT
	 (1) Prepare the Workplace
	     Get specified tools, material
	     Arrange for best efficiency
	 (2) Prepare Yourself
	     Breakdown job for instruction
	     List the Important Steps
	     List Key Points in each step
	     Plan the instruction
	 (3) Prepare the Learner
	     Put him at ease
	     State job, Learn his experience
	     Interest him in learning
	     Explain use and care of tools,
	       equipment, safeguards, etc.
	     Position him for learning
		GET THE FACTS
		 Review the records
		 What rules and plant customs
		   apply?
		 Talk with individuals, get opinions
		   and feelings.
		
		 WEIGH THE FACTS
		 Fit facts together
		 Check for gaps, omissions,
		   contradictions
		 Consider their bearing upon each
		   other
		 Check against company practices
		   and policies
		
		 MAKE THE DECISION
		 Consider effect upon individual,
		   group, production

STEP 3—CORRECT THE PROBLEM

| **DEVELOP THE IMPROVED WAY**
 Eliminate unnecessary details
 Combine where practical
 Rearrange for better sequence
 Simplify necessary details

 RECORD PROPOSED CORRECTION
 Make a Flow Chart of new method
 Make a Flow Diagram of new method

 PUT IT INTO EFFECT
 Get final approval of all concerned on:
 Safety, Quality, Quantity, Cost | **INSTRUCT THE LEARNER**
 Instruct
   Tell, Show, Illustrate one step at a
     time, stressing Key Points
   Test with "W" questions
 Try out learners performance
   Have him do the job
   Have him repeat, Telling what he is
     Showing, stressing Key Points
   Test him with "WHY" questions
 Put him on his own
   Stress quality and safety
   Encourage questions about job
   Tell him who to ask for help | **TAKE ACTION**
 Consider time and places
 Explain this action
   Why it is best for him
   Advantages and benefits
 Secure understanding and acceptance
 Put into effect
   Consider feelings and attitudes
 Notify all concerned |

STEP 4—CHECK AND EVALUATE

Follow up to see what the change or correction has been made.

What improvements do the records show in Quality, Quantity, Safety, Cost?

Consider the Human Angle. Note changes in attitudes and relationships.

Inform all those concerned of progress and results of the action or correction.

Look for ways to prevent a recurrence of this problem.

OUTLINE FOR SOLVING MECHANICAL PROBLEMS

When it Involves	ACTION

When it Involves (left column) / **ACTION** (right column)

METHODS — ANALYZE THE OVERALL JOB OR SITUATION

Make a Flow Chart

List routing or travel of a part, material or paper.

LAYOUT

Show relationship to prior and subsequent operations or situations.

Question the job or situation as a whole.

Make a Flow Diagram

TOOLS

Show layout and locations of work stations, equipment, aisles, etc.

Study for better production efficiency and for possible causes of problems.

MACHINES — ANALYZE SPECIFIC JOB OR SITUATION

Make a breakdown of the method of doing the job or of the situation

List all details including:

EQUIPMENT

Material handling

Machine work

Hand work

MATERIALS — QUESTION ALL DETAILS TO LOCATE PROBLEM SOURCES

WHY is it necessary?

WHAT is its purpose?

WHERE should it be done?

WHEN should it be done?

WHO is best qualified to do it?

HOW is the best way to do it?

STEP 1—ISOLATE THE PROBLEM

1. <u>State the problem</u>

   Is it MECHANICAL pertaining to Things and Places?

   Is it PEOPLE who Don't Know—Can't Do—Don't Care—Won't Do?

2. <u>Give proof or Evidence of the Problem</u>

MECHANICAL	PEOPLE who:		
	Don't Know Can't Do	Don't Care Won't Do	
Schedules	Productivity	Attitude	
Rework and Scrap	Work habits	Interest	
Tool wear and breakage	Skill	Job satisfaction	
Equipment breakdowns	Ability	Personality	
Accidents	Safety	Physical Condition	
Records and paperwork	Responsibilities	Health	

3. <u>Explore the Cause</u>

Method   Job assignment

Tools   Faulty instructions

Equipment   Personality situation

Material   Insufficient skill

Layout   Human relations

Design   Unsafe acts

Standards

Unsafe condition.

(Use questions: Why did this happen?, Where?, When?, Who is responsible?)

4. <u>Draw Conclusions</u>

   Weigh causes

   Is the difficulty MECHANICAL? PEOPLE? or BOTH?

   Decide on plan of solution.

ISOLATE THE PROBLEM

This problem concerns: QUALITY ◯ QUANTITY ◯ SAFETY ◯ COST ◯ PEOPLE ◯

Exactly what is the problem?

PROOF or EVIDENCE of the PROBLEM

Involving:	When it is **MECHANICAL** Things and Places.		When it is **PEOPLE** Who: Don't Know - Can't Do - Don't Care - Won't Do
Behind schedule by		per	Productivity is
Rework is up by		per	Work habits are
Scrap is up by		per	Job interest is
Tool breakage is up by		per	General attitude is
Machine down time is		per	Workmanship is
Accident rate is up by		per	Complains are
Set-up time is		per	Attendance is
Paperwork is increased by		per	Job satisfaction is

EXPLORE THE CAUSE

The above problems are caused by... ↱		The above problems are caused by... ↱	
Job Method		Incorrect job assignment	
Layout		Faulty Instruction and follow-up	
Tools, fixtures, dies, gages, etc.		Insufficient skill and experience	
Machines and Equipment		Poor human relations	
Materials and Pparts		Personality situation	
Product Design		Basic wants threatened	
Housekeeping and working conditions		Health and physical fitness	
Unsafe conditions		Unsafe acts	

CONCLUSION

This problem is MECHANICAL... ◯, or it involves PEOPLE... ◯, or BOTH... ◯.

SIMPLIFY or IMPROVE the JOB

STEP 2—QUESTION EVERY DETAIL

We question the "DO" detail or details first because if they are unnecessary then there is no use to question the rest of the operation.
If this is necessary, then continue the questioning in the regular manner.

"MAKE READY" and "PUT AWAY" details.

The greatest opportunity for improvements lies in these details.
These details consist of the time and effort used in getting the job ready and after is has been down to clear it away. It is getting the necessary materials and supplies and placing them, and putting the finished product aside after the operation. It also includes getting the trucks, racks, pans, boxes, skids, etc.
The movement of material without definite work accomplishment is either:

MAKE READY   PUT AWAY   OR   WASTE

These very definitely should be questioned with improvements in mind.

Types of questions to be asked.

1. WHY IS IT NECESSARY?
   We ask this question of each detail to distinguish necessary details from those that are unnecessary or doubtful.
   This is the most important question and yet the hardest to get answered.

2. WHAT IS ITS PURPOSE?
   This is the check question to WHY is it necessary. We want to learn if the detail has a useful purpose or adds to quality. If it does not, we will reconsider its necessity.
   If the detail is found unnecessary, then continue with other questions.

3. WHERE SHOULD IT BE DONE?
   Where is the best place or location to do the detail? Why is it done there? Where else could it be done? Could it be combined with another?

4. WHEN SHOULD IT BE DONE?
   We ask this questions to find the best time to do each detail. What details must it follow and what detail must it precede? Why is it done then? At what other time could it be done? Are the details in proper sequence? Can it be done simultaneously with another?

5. WHO IS BEST QUALIFIED TO DO IT?
   We ask this question to learn who is best qualified from the stand-point of skill, experience, or physical strength. Can women be used here? Can "old timers" be used instead of young men?

6. HOW IS THE BEST WAY TO DO IT?
   We ask this question only after asking WHERE?, WHEN?, and WHO?
   We want to learn if there is a better way to do the detail. Can it be done easier and safer? Can the layout of the work station be improved? Are proper tools and equipment used?

List your IDEAS and THOUGHTS arising from these questions on the breakdown sheet in the column marked "NOTES and IDEAS." It is from these that the new method is developed.

STEP 2—PREPARE FOR SOLUTION

If its MECHANICAL	If its PEOPLE	Who
Methods, Layout, Tools, Materials, Equipment	Don't Know Can't Do	Don't Care Won't Do
Improve — Method for better way	Improve — Knowledge - Skill - Productivity	Improve — Attitude - Behavior

<u>Analyze</u>
 	
(1) Overall Situation
    Flow Chart
    Flow Diagram
 	
Question overall job
	<u>Get Ready to Instruct</u>
	
	1. Prepare the Workplaces
	    Have everything ready
	    Have workplace set up
	      properly
		<u>Get the Facts</u>
		
		Review the records
		    What rules and
		      plant customs
		      apply
		
		Talk with individuals
		    concerned
		
		Get opinions
		    and feelings

(2) Specific Situation
    Method Breakdown
    Layout Diagram
	2. Prepare Yourself
	    Breakdown job for instruction
	      List important steps
	      List key points
	      Plan the Instruction
		<u>Weigh the Facts</u>
		
		Fit facts together
		Any gaps, omissions,
		    or contradictions
		Consider their bear-
		    ing upon each
		    other
		Check against Com-
		    pany Practices
		    and Policies

<u>Question each detail</u>
 	
Why is it necessary
What is its purpose?
Where is it to be done?
When is it to be done?
Who is best qualified?
How is the best way?
	3. Prepare the Learner
	    Put him at ease
	    Name job. Show finished part
	    Learn what he knows about
	      the job
	    Interest him in learning the
	      job
	    Explain use and care of:
	      tools, gauges, equipment,
	      safeguards
	    Position him for learning
		<u>Make the Decision</u>
		
		Consider effect upon
		    individual, group,
		    production

SIMPLIFY OR IMPROVE THE JOB
STEP 3—DEVELOP THE NEW METHOD

This step is actually a reasoning process. Here you use the answers to the questions asked in Step 2, together with the IDEAS which you jotted down on the breakdown sheet to finally arrive at a possible improvement.
If possible you should tryout the new method.

We can make improvements only when details are Eliminated, Combined, Rearranged, and Simplified. As the new method is developed, write the details step by step in the "Proposed Method" column of the breakdown sheet.

ELIMINATE UNNECESSARY DETAILS
 We eliminate details to avoid unnecessary use of manpower, machines, tools, materials, and time.

 The answers to "WHY" and "WHAT" lead us to eliminating unnecessary details. The answer to "WHY" must justify the existence of the detail.

COMBINE DETAILS in whole or in part, where practical.
 Possibilities for combining details are often discovered by finding the best place, best time, and the best person to do them.

 Combining details often reduces the total time as the new combination may be done in less time than was formerly needed to do the two separately.

 All transportations, delays, inspections, and storages are eliminated between two or more details the moment they are combined.
 The answers to "WHERE," "WHEN," and "WHO" are leads for combining.

REARRANGE DETAILS for better sequence where practical.
 Here the details are moved from one to another location in the sequence.

 We rearrange details to reduce handlings, back-tracking, delays, accidents hazards, and to improve maintenance possibilities or working conditions.

 The answers to "WHERE," "WHEN," and "WHO" also give leads for rearranging.

SIMPLIFY all necessary details
 After we have made every possible Elimination, Combination and Change of Sequence, the development of "HOW is the best way to do the job" is now considered. It is the last phase of a development and should be applied after all other steps are completed.
 The answer to "HOW is the best way to do it" leads to simplifying.

 Avoid unnecessary non-productive motions. Make the work easier and safer. Preposition materials, tools, and equipment at the best places in the proper work area. Use gravity feed hoppers and drop delivery chutes. Let both hands do useful work. Use jigs and fixtures instead of hands to hold work.

 To reduce the time necessary to acquire skill, the fundamental principles of motion economy should be studied and used.

STEP II
QUESTION DETAILS

STEP III
DEVELOP A NEW METHOD

WHY
is it necessary?

WHAT
is it purpose?

→

ELIMINATE
unnecessary
jobs: steps: details

WHERE
should it be done?

WHEN
should it be done?

WHO
is best qualified to do it?

→

COMBINE
to reduce

REARRANGE
for better sequence
to reduce
handlings & backtracking

HOW
is the best way to do it?

→

SIMPLIFY
Motions
Layouts
Tools
Materials handling

JOB METHODS BREAKDOWN WORK SHEET

PRODUCT___Radio Shields_____ No._____ DATE_____ CHARTED BY _Bill Brown___
OPERATION_Inspect, Assemble, Rivet, Stamp and Pack___ No.___ DEPT. Rivet & Pack__ Sheet___ of___

No.	Details of Proposed Method	News	IDEAS Write them down — Don't trust your memory
1			
2			
3	This Part used in Step 1	Here	
4			
5			
6			
7			
8			
10			Here
11			
12			
13			
14			

Write down the
IDEAS you get
from questioning

List details of the
proposed method

STEP 3—CORRECT THE PROBLEM

MECHANICAL	PEOPLE	
Develop new method	1. Instruct the learner	Take Action
Eliminate unnecessary details		Consider time and place
		Explain Action
Combine details where practical	2. Tryout performance	Benefits to him
Rearrange details for better sequence		Put into effect
	3. Put him on his own	Notify all concerned
Simplify all of the necessary details		
Record proposed correction		
Put it into effect		

STEP 4—CHECK AND EVALUATE RESULTS

Follow up to see that the change or correction has been made.
What improvements do the records show in Quality, Quantity, Safety, Cost?
Consider the Human Angle. Not changes in attitudes and relationships.
Inform all those concerned of progress and results of the action or correction.
Look for ways to prevent a recurrence of this problem.

DID YOUR ACTION HELP PRODUCTION?

PRACTICE DEMONSTRATION

Procedure for presenting a Mechanical Problem

1. Describe the problem. (Tell in a natural narrative manner)
   What is the problem?
   Who is affected?
   What are the effects of the problem?
   When and where did it start?

2. Explain how the problem was isolated.

   Use large chart or board. Members to copy data on their sheets.

3. Explain how Step 2 was used to analyze the overall situation.

   Use large Flow Chart or board showing present method. (Members copy)

   Use Flow Diagrams if needed to show overall layout. (Copy on board)

4. Explain how Step 2 was used to analyze the specific situation.

   Use large Job Methods Breakdown Chart or board showing present method.
   Members copy.

   Use the questioning method to demonstrate how facts were discovered, which
   enable you to develop a new method, thus correcting the problem.
   (Members do not participate at this time)

5. Explain how Step 3 was used in developing a new method or making a
   correction of the problem.

   If Flow Chart or Flow Diagrams furnished sufficient facts to make the
   correction then:

   > Use large Flow Chart showing the proposed situations. Members copy.

   > Use the Flow Diagram (board) showing the proposed layout.

   If analysis of the specific situation was needed to make the correction then:

   > Complete the Methods Breakdown using chart or board showing the
   > proposed or corrected method. Members copy.

6. Explain how Step 4 will be used in this problem.

   When and where will the correction be made?

   Who will be notified of the correction?

   What facts and data will be collected to prove the problem is solved?

   Could this problem have been prevented?   How?

THE "SMITH" PROBLEM

Brown, the drill press operator in Dept. "A" was working at his job, drilling the #1 hole in angle plates.

He had cut his finger while moving tote pans of material to the work area.

The standard specifications of the job called for gauging one piece in twenty for size. Brown did this and, although the pain from his finger was diverting his attention, all that he gauged seemed good.

He therefore had no indication that the drill was dull, nor that the machine wasn't running at the correct speed. It was just as the set-up man had left it. By mid-morning he had completed five tote pans for a total of 100 pieces.

Smith, the Supervisor, suddenly called Brown to his desk and reprimanded him for carelessness in his work.

Brown was angry and felt discouraged. He told the supervisor he was going home at noon.

Smith, the Supervisor, was worried because Dept. "B" needed the work now or they would have to stop production. The Inspector had told him that a great many of the angle plates were off specifications.

HUMAN PROBLEMS IN METHOD IMPROVEMENTS

Many difficulties are encountered in dealing with people when attempting to present or install any new IDEA or METHOD, but two human failings have been responsible for stopping more improvements from being put to work than any others, namely:

        (a) RESISTANCE to new ideas or changes

        (b) RESENTMENT of criticism

RESISTANCE to new ideas or changes

Every time a method is changed people are involved and serious consideration must be given to the effect of this change upon them. Occasionally the savings involved in the new improvement is not worth the upset in human relations caused.

The basis of this resistance has little to do with reasoning. It is an emotional reaction. It is FEAR.

They fear:

      Upset of routines
      Change of work habits
      Effect upon their production
      Change in working conditions
      Their ability to learn the new method

There is a tendency to build "empires."

We defend past practices, customs, traditions, work methods and habits. We often hear, "Why change this?" "We have been doing this for years!" etc.

This resistance to change may happen any time, such as when:

      1. Processing the proposals
      2. Putting them into effect
            Supervisors may be skeptical
            Employees fear the effects

How can this resistance be overcome?

Tell people in advance about changes that will affect them.

Tell them WHY: Present the idea or change in a clear, simple, concise manner.

      Make a trial run of the new method demonstrating advantages.

      Present facts to prove the benefits expected, such as:

            Figures of savings

            Charts, Diagrams, Breakdown sheets, Sketches, etc.

      Clarify the effect upon persons involved. Give assurance that:

            The job will be simpler, safer, easier and more comfortable

            Possibilities of accomplishments are undisturbed

            When operations or jobs are eliminated, other important work will be found

RESENTMENT of criticism

Often someone may interpret your search for a better method as a personal criticism. All concerned should understand that the proposed change is not a criticism of past methods, or of those persons who originally proposed or installed the present method, but that it is a constructive search for a better way to get out quality production, in sufficient quantity and on time, at a more satisfactory cost.

Remember that people do not like to be told that they are wrong, so in discussing any new method or change, refrain from inferring personal criticism.

Other factors to be overcome when making methods improvements:

Reluctance to assume the initiative; Tendency to overrate the importance of the job; Reluctance to admit that what we do is unnecessary or nonessential.

MAKE A JOB BREAKDOWN SHEET

In order to more easily train a new employee it is important that the instructor be able to break a job down to it's most Important Steps and Key Points. Creating a Job Breakdown Sheet will assist in the trainer.

In order to accurately fill out a Job Breakdown Sheet, the trainer must ask himself the following questions:

- *Why is it necessary?*
    To <u>clearly organize the job</u> in one's mind.

- *What is its purpose?*
    To <u>know what you are going to put over; how much;</u> and <u>in what order</u>.

- *Where should it be done?*
    Right on the job.

- *When should it be done?*
    Every time you have any instructing to do. (Once completed, file for future use.)

- *Who should do it?*
    The person who is to do the instructing. Supervisor—Foreman—lead person, etc.

- *How is the best way to make a job breakdown?*
    Here is a quick, simple way to do it:

*1. The first thing you do is to fill in the headings.

*2. Next you list the

Start doing the job until there is

Then write it in this space as step

Continue the job, listing the important steps in the consecutive spaces.

*3. Start doing the job again. Do the first step. Pick out the Key Points.

List them briefly opposite Step 1 in the proper space. Continue with the job, doing each step, picking out the key points,

JOB BREAKDOWN SHEET FOR TRAINING MAN ON NEW JOB

Operation: __SET UP TO DRILL #1 HOLE__   Part: __DRILL PRESS #55__

IMPORTANT STEPS IN THE OPERATION	KEY POINTS
Step: A logical segment of the operation when something happens to ADVANCE the work.	Key Point: Anything in a shop that might — Make or break the job. Make the work easier to do, i.e., bit of special information.
1 GET SPECIFICATION SHEET AND TOOLS FOR THE JOB	FROM TOOL CRIB CHECK TOOLS WITH SPECS
2 SET MACHINE SPEED	ADJUST BELTS AN DPULLEYS
3 SET UP MACHINE	INSERT PROPER DRILL AND TIGHTEN ADJUST TO HEIGH AND SET STOPS
4 INSTRUCT THE OPERATOR	FOLLOW JOB INSTRUCTION SHEET USE JOB INSTRUCTION TECHNIQUES
5 GAGE FIRST FEW PIECES	USE PLUG GATE #3654

* <u>Breakdowns</u> are <u>not</u> micro-motion studies, job descriptions, nor instruction sheets for workers. They are just simple, common-sense outlines that you make of the job, so you will not overlook or miss anything when you instruct another on that job.

JOB BREAKDOWN SHEET FOR TRAINING MAN ON NEW JOB

Operation _____ Drill #1 Hole _____ Part _____ Angle Plates #35 _____

IMPORTANT STEPS IN THE OPERATION Step: A logical segment of the operation when something happens to ADVANCE the work.	KEY POINTS Key Point: Anything in a shop that might — Make or break the job. Injure the worker. Make the work easier to do, i.e., "knack," "trick," special timing, bit of special information.
Place piece in fixture and lock	Face down Angle to left Clamp securely
Slide fixture under drill	To back stop
Drill to stop	Use gentle pressure Release drill
Withdraw fixture	Pull towards you
Remove piece and dump chips	Unclamp Turn fixture over to remove piece and chips
Place finished piece aside	In pan Angle to left
Gauge with Go—No-Go Gauge	One per pan of 20

JUST WHAT AM I TRYING TO ACCOMPLISH

ALL THE FACTS IN THIS PROBLEM

CHECKLIST AGAINST POSSIBLE ACTIONS

POSSIBLE ACTIONS	PRACTICES & POLICIES?	ACCOMPLISH OBJECTIVES?	EFFECT UPON INDIVIDUAL?	EFFECT UPON GROUP?	EFFECT UPON PRODUCTION?

FINAL ACTION TAKEN

JOB METHODS BREAKDOWN WORK SHEET

PRODUCT __Radio Shields__   No. _____   **CHARTED BY** Bill Brown

OPERATION __Inspect, Assemble, Rivet, Stamp and Pack__   No. _____   DATE _____   Sheet ____ of ____

     DEPT. __Rivet & Pack__

No.	Details of Proposed Method	TIME IN MIN	DISTANCE IN FEET	News	WHY	WHERE	WHEN	WHO	HOW	IDEAS Write them down — Don't trust your memory	Eliminate	Combine	Rearrange	Simplify
1.	Put pile of copper sheets in right jig			Boxes placed on table by Handler										
2.	Put pile of brass sheets in left jig													
3.	Pick up 1 copper sheet in right hand and 1 brass sheet in left hand													
4.	Inspect both sheets			Scratches and dents. Drop scrap through slots.										
5.	Assemble sheets and place in fixture			Fixtures line up sheets and locates rivet holes										
6.	Rivet the 2 bottom corners													
7.	Remove, reverse, and place sheets													
8.	Rivet the 2 top corners													
9.	Place Shield in front of fixture. Repeat No. 3 to No. 9 - 19 times													
10.	Put 20 Shields in shipping case — 200/case			Cases placed by Handler										
11.	Carry full cases to Packing Dept.			By Handler with hand truck										
12.	Close, stencil cases			Check inspection by Packer										
13.	Write weight on delivery slip			200 Shields in case, uniform weight										
14.	Set cases aside for shipment													

91

JOB METHODS BREAKDOWN WORK SHEET

PRODUCT _____
OPERATION _____ No. _____
No. _____
DATE _____
DEPT. _____
CHARTED BY _____
Sheet ____ of ____

No.	Details of Proposed Method	TIME IN MIN	DISTANCE IN FEET	News	WHY	WHERE	WHEN	WHO	HOW	IDEAS Write them down — Don't trust your memory	Eliminate	Combine	Rearrange	Simplify
1.														
2.														
3.														
4.														
5.														
6.														
7.														
8.														
9.														
10.														
11.														
12.														
13.														
14.														

JOB METHODS BREAKDOWN

From: ___Joe Smith___ Department: __Rivet & Pack__ Date: _02/02/44_
Part Number: ___#104___ Part Name: ___Radio Shield___
Operation Number: ____#119____ Operation Name: __Riveting Radio Shields__

No.	Details of PRESENT METHOD	NOTES and IDEAS Write down at once	Details of PROPOSED METHOD
1	Walk to get Copper sheets	Place at bench, remove walking	At work station, reach over and get Copper sheets
2	Place sheets on bench for inspection	Combine with inspection of Brass sheets	Create jigs to place Copper sheets in to hold a large amount until inspection
3	Inspect Copper sheets	Combine with Brass sheet inspection using jigs	Grab one of each sheet from jigs and inspect together
4	Walk back to replace excess Copper sheets with bunch	Place at bench, remove walking	
5	Walk to get Brass sheets	Place at bench, remove walking	At work station, reach over to get Brass sheets
6	Place sheets on bench for inspection	Combine with inspection of Copper sheets	Create jigs to place Brass sheets in to hold a large amount until inspection
7	Inspect Brass sheets	Combine with Copper sheet inspection using jigs	Grab one of each sheet from jigs and inspect together
8			
9			
10			
11			
12			

JOB METHODS BREAKDOWN

From: _____ Department: _____ Date:_____
Part Number: _____ Part Name: _____
Operation Number: _____ Operation Name: _____

No.	Details of PRESENT METHOD	NOTES and IDEAS Write down at once	Details of PROPOSED METHOD

MAKE A FLOW CHART

Experience has shown that a Flow Chart can be used to great advantages when studying a situation where a change is contemplated.

It shows the present routing of the subject and its relationship to prior and subsequent operations, transportations, inspections, delays, and storages.

The subject may be a part, an assembly, a material, a person, or a paper form. Most cases involve the study of a part or an assembly.

One of the important sections of a Flow Chart is the "Symbols section." These symbols are used to graphically show what is happening to the subject being studied.
Extra emphasis can be obtained by drawing a connection line from symbol to symbol, thus highlighting such costly items as excessive transportations, delays, and storages.
Extra attention may be drawn to these high cost items by using a color effect, such as drawing different color lines or by filling in the symbol blocks in color.

Definitions covering the meaning of the symbols used is found on the next page.

Here is a quick, easy way to make a Flow Chart:

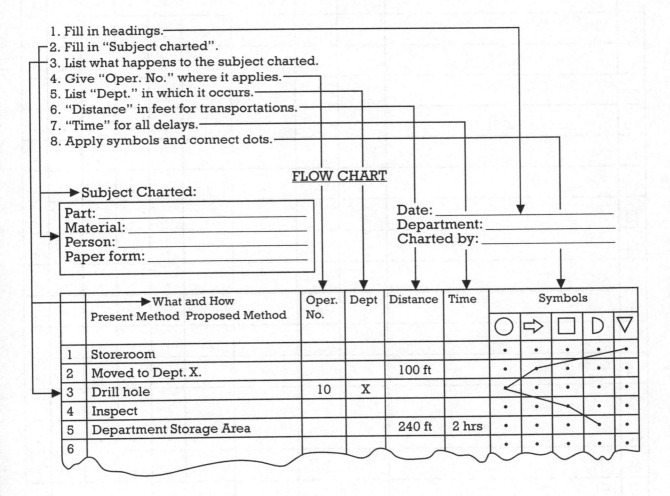

1. Fill in headings.
2. Fill in "Subject charted".
3. List what happens to the subject charted.
4. Give "Oper. No." where it applies.
5. List "Dept." in which it occurs.
6. "Distance" in feet for transportations.
7. "Time" for all delays.
8. Apply symbols and connect dots.

FLOW CHART

Subject Charted:

Part: _____
Material: _____
Person: _____
Paper form: _____

Date: _____
Department: _____
Charted by: _____

	What and How Present Method Proposed Method	Oper. No.	Dept	Distance	Time	Symbols				
						◯	⇨	▢	D	▽
1	Storeroom					·	·	·	·	·
2	Moved to Dept. X.			100 ft		·	·	·	·	·
3	Drill hole	10	X			·	·	·	·	·
4	Inspect					·	·	·	·	·
5	Department Storage Area			240 ft	2 hrs	·	·	·	·	·
6						·	·	·	·	·

FLOW CHART

Subject Charted:

Part: _____
Material: _____
Person: _____
Paper form: _____

Date: _____
Department: _____
Charted by: _____

	What and How Present Method Proposed Method	Oper. No.	Dept	Distance	Time	Symbols ◯	⇨	□	D	▽
1						•	•	•	•	•
2						•	•	•	•	•
3						•	•	•	•	•
4						•	•	•	•	•
5						•	•	•	•	•
6						•	•	•	•	•
7						•	•	•	•	•
8						•	•	•	•	•
9						•	•	•	•	•
10						•	•	•	•	•
11						•	•	•	•	•
12						•	•	•	•	•
13						•	•	•	•	•
14						•	•	•	•	•
15						•	•	•	•	•
16						•	•	•	•	•
17						•	•	•	•	•
18						•	•	•	•	•
19						•	•	•	•	•
20						•	•	•	•	•
21						•	•	•	•	•
22						•	•	•	•	•
23						•	•	•	•	•

STANDARD DEFINITION OF SYMBOLS

We have adopted the standardized A.S.M.E. symbols. They are as follows:

Classification	Predominant Results	Symbol and Definition

Operation — **Produces**

○

An operation occurs when:
(a) An object is intentionally changed in any of its physical or chemical characteristics.
(b) It is assembled or dissembled from another object.
(c) It is arranged or prepared for another operation, transportation, inspection, storage.

An operation also occurs when:
(a) Information is given or received.
(b) When planning or calculating takes place.

Transportation — **Moves**

⇒

A transportation occurs when an object is moved from one place to another, except when such movements are a part of the operation or are caused by the operator at work station during an operation or an inspection.

Inspection — **Verified**

□

An inspection occurs when an object is examined for identification or is verified for quality or quantity in any of its characteristics.

Delay — **Interference**

D

A delay occurs to an object when conditions, except those which intentionally change the physical or chemical characteristics of the object, do not permit or require immediate performance of the next planned action.

Storage — **Keeps**

▽

A storage occurs when an object is kept and protected against unauthorized removal.

Combined Activity

Operation-Inspection   Storage-Inspection
◯⃞   ▽⃞

When it is desired to show activities performed either concurrently or by the same operator at the same work station, the symbols for these activities are combined.

97

PRESENT METHOD LAYOUT

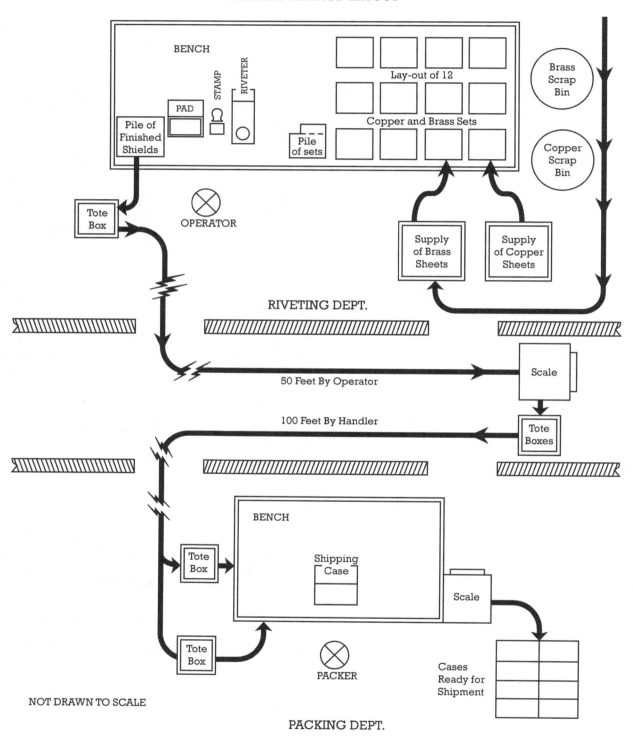

NOT DRAWN TO SCALE

The mind like a parachute, functions only when open

Publications from Enna

From Enna's new classics by Shigeo Shingo to our books and training packages regarding operational excellence, Enna provides companies with the foundation of knowledge and practical implementation ideas that will ensure your efforts to internalize process improvement. Reach your vision and mission with the expertise within these world-class texts. Call toll-free (866) 249-7348, visit us on the web at www.enna.com to order, or request our free product catalog.

Enjoy the rest of the books in our T.W.I. Training Series:

Job Instruction: Sessions Outline and Materials

Job Instruction, a short, intensive training program, was developed in order to provide skills in leadership to new and experienced supervisors alike. Contained within the Job Instruction book are samples, scenarios, and discussion topics which give you the tools necessary to properly instruct new workers and do away with waste and accidents, as well as cut down the time it takes to get a new worker 'up to speed' on his job.
ISBN 978-1-897363-92-8 | 2009 | $34.99 | Item: **922**

Job Methods: Sessions Outline and Materials

In teaching you the method behind the job and how to properly break down a job into its most fundamental parts, this book aims to teach you how to reduce wasteful behavior and wasteful steps within a job. The training material within provides you with worksheets, forms and sample scenarios to give you practice in scrutinizing and simplifying jobs.
ISBN 978-1-897363-93-5 | 2009 | $34.99 | Item: **923**

Job Relations: Sessions Outline and Materials

Job Relations was developed in order to provide management with a tool whereby supervisors could acquire skills in leadership. Contained within the Job Relations book are sample scenarios, discussion topics and instructional diagrams that relate the supervisor and his subordinates, show the dynamic of such a relationship and provide a way of looking at and dealing with these relationships that will benefit everyone in the company.
ISBN 978-1-897363-94-2 | 2009 | $34.99 | Item: **924**

Union Job Relations: Sessions Outline and Materials

Union Job Relations was developed concurrently with Job Relations in order to provide stewards with a way to acquire skills in leadership within their company and union. Contained within the Union Job Relations book are sample scenarios, discussion topics and instructional diagrams that relate the steward to his union, supervisors and the union members he is responsible for, shows the dynamic of such relationships and provide a way of looking at and dealing with these relationships that will benefit everyone in the company.
ISBN 978-1-897363-95-9 | 2009 | $34.99 | Item: **925**

To Order: Enna Corp., 1602 Carolina Street, Unit B3, Bellingham, WA 98229

Program Development Institute

The Program Development Institute was established in order to train people in setting up and implementing an entire training program within their company. Enclosed are worksheets, examples and practice problems to assist in developing the program as a training coordinator. With this book you will learn how to step back and look at the company as a whole, before implementing training and improvements.
ISBN 978-1-897363-96-6 | 2009 | $34.99 | Item: **926**

Problem Solving Training: Sessions Outline and Materials

The Problem Solving workbook instructs on how to properly Isolate, Breakdown, Question and Solve problems. From detailing just how you know you have a problem to charts and diagrams that will assist you in solving the problem, this book is a must read for anyone who deals with production on a daily basis.
ISBN 978-1-926537-00-9 | 2009 | $34.99 | Item: **927**

Bulletin Series

Based on the simple premise that in order to function there has to be an organized structure that recognizes that ongoing training is an investment that will always pay for itself the T.W.I. Bulletin Series is packed with ideas, concepts, and methods that will produce results. Contained within are bulletins that will assist in selecting supervisors, strengthening management and achieving continuous results.
ISBN 978-1-897363-91-1 | 2008 | $34.99 | Item: **914**

Other Books by Enna

Mistaken Kanbans

Let Mistaken Kanbans be your roadmap to guide you through the steps necessary to implement and successful Kanban System. This book will help you to not only understand the complexities of a Kanban System but gives you the tools necessary, and the guidance through real-life lessons learned, to avoid disastrous consequences related to the improper use of such systems.
ISBN 978-1-926537-10-8 | 2009 | $27.99 | Item: **919**

The Toyota Mindset

From the brilliant mind of a legend in the LEAN manufacturing world comes the reasoning behind the importance of using your intellect, challenging your workers and why continuous improvement is so important. For anyone who wishes to gain insight into how the Toyota Production System came to be or wants to know more about the person behind TPS this book is a must read!
ISBN 978-1-926537-11-5 | 2009 | $34.99 | Item: **920**

Phone: 1+ (360) 306-5369   **Fax:** (905) 481-0756   **Email:** info@enna.com

The Toyota Way in Sales and Marketing

Many companies today are trying to implement the ideas and principles of Lean into non-traditional environments, such as service centers, sales organizations and transactional environments. In this book Mr. Ishizaka provides insight on how to apply Lean operational principles and Kaizen to these dynamic and complicated environments.

ISBN 978-1-926537-08-5 | 2009 | $28.99 | Item: **918**

Training Packages

5S Training Package

Our 5S Solution Packages will help your company create a sustainable 5S program that will turn your shop floor around and put you ahead of the competition. All of the benefits that come from Lean Manufacturing are built upon a strong foundation of 5S. Enna's solution packages will show you how to implement and sustain an environment of continuous improvement.

Version 1: Sort, Straighten, Sweep, Standardize and Sustain
ISBN 978-0-973750-90-4 | 2005 | $429.99 | Item: **12**
Version 2: Sort, Set In Order, Shine, Standardize and Sustain
ISBN 978-1-897363-25-6 | 2006 | $429.99 | Item: **17**

Study Mission to Japan

We are excited to present an exclusive trip to the birthplace of Lean. We provide a one-week unique tour at a reasonable all-inclusive price that will guide you to a better understanding of Lean Manufacturing principles. Enna has exclusive access to Toyota and Toyota suppliers due to our publications of Dr. Shigeo Shingo's classic manuscripts. You will have one-on-one access to

Japanese Lean Executives and learn from their experiences and solutions. We also offer custom private tours for executive management teams over 12 people. Join us on our next tour by visiting www.enna.com/japantrip and register on-line or by telephone at: +1 (360) 306-5369

To Order:
Mail orders and checks to:
Enna Products Corporation
ATTN: Order Processing
1602 Carolina Street, Unit B3
Bellingham, WA 98229, USA
Phone: +1 (360) 306-5369 • Fax: (905) 481-0756
Email: info@enna.com

We accept checks and all major credit cards.
Notice: All prices are in US Dollars and are subject to change without notice.

To Order: Enna Corp., 1602 Carolina Street, Unit B3, Bellingham, WA 98229

CPSIA information can be obtained
at www.ICGtesting.com
Printed in the USA
FSOW03n1231210416
19505FS

9 781926 537